EICHER GUIDE

WALKING WITH
THE BUDDHA

Buddhist Pilgrimages in India

EICHER GOODEARTH LIMITED, New Delhi

Supported by

Ministry of Tourism, Government of India.

AN EICHER GOODEARTH PUBLICATION

Copyright © 1999 Eicher Goodearth Limited, New Delhi
ISBN 81-900601-6-3

Editor and Publisher: Swati Mitra

Designer: Sagarmoy Paul
Assistant Editor: Himanjali Sankar
Research Associate: M N Rajesh

Text: Varsha Rani, Subhadra Sengupta, M N Rajesh,
Lavanya Kondepudi, Shantum Seth
Photographs: Benoy K Behl (pp 4, 42Below, 144-148, 153Above)
Chinmoy Basu (pp.10, 18, 20B, 34, 39 inset, 39B, 43A, 45, 48A, 50B, 68A, 122, 151A, 169)
Mimansak (pp. 19, 20 inset, 22, 96A, 97B, 98-103, 114B, 115, 117A, 119M, 124-126)
Sagarmoy Paul (pp. 31A, 47, 53B, 152B)
Swati Mitra (pp. 23, 71A, 72A, 73, 92, 95B, 96M, 96B, 97A, 97M, 139A, 141, 150)
Varsha Rani (pp.3, 6A, 8B, 12B, 14, 17B, 20A, 24B, 26, 27, 31B- 33, 36-38 inset, 48B, 50A, 52,
58-67, 69, 71B, 74-91, 94, 95A, 104-113, 114A, 116, 118-120, 123, 129-130, 132-137,
139B, 140, 142, 153)
Map Advisor: Lt Gen (Retd) S M Chadha
Editorial Advisor: Chuden Tshering Misra
Maps: Charanjit Singh, V Murali
Secretarial Assistance: C K Sathian

Great care has been taken in the compilation, updation and validation
of information, and every effort has been made to ensure that all
information is as up-to-date as possible at the time of going to press.
Details like telephone and fax numbers, opening hours, prices and
travel information may change. However, the Publishers are not
responsible for errors, if any, and their consequences.

The Publishers would be happy to receive suggestions and corrections
for inclusion in the next edition. Please write to Head of Publishing,
Eicher Goodearth Ltd, Eicher House, 12 Commercial Complex,
Greater Kailash II (Masjid Moth), New Delhi 110 048.

This publication has been supported by
Ministry of Tourism, Government of India.

Printed by Ajanta Offset & Packaging Ltd, New Delhi
on behalf of Eicher Goodearth Ltd

Price: Rs 250

CONTENTS

Queen Mahamaya's dream. Panel from Sanchi,
2nd century AD.

LIFE OF THE BUDDHA

Once upon a time, over twentyfive centuries ago, Kapilavastu, the capital of the Sakyas was in a festive mood. Mahamaya, the chief queen of King Suddhodana, had a dream in which a magnificent white elephant with a lotus in his trunk appeared and entered her side. The sixtyfour Brahman soothsayers who were invited to interpret the queen's dream prophesied that she would give birth to an illustrious son who would either be a world conqueror or a world renouncer.

A cavalcade goes forth to witness the Lord.
Panel from Sanchi, 1st century BC.

On the auspicious full moon day of *Vaisakha*, in 566 BC in Lumbini grove, just outside Kapilavastu, the young prince was born. He was named Siddhartha Gautama (*Siddhartha* meaning one who has achieved his purpose, *Gautama* being the name of his *gotra* or clan).

The Hindu kingdom of the Sakyas was located in the foothills of the Himalayas. Beyond these were the snowy ranges, home to a number of recluse sages. One of them was Asita, who was invited by Suddhodana on the birth of his son. Much to the bewilderment of the assembled courtiers, Asita proclaimed that the young prince would become a universal teacher if he ever experienced suffering.

Left:
The child Buddha, Mayadevi Temple, Lumbini

Right:
Queen Mahamaya stands on a lotus and clasps a branch of the sacred sal tree, the tree under which the Buddha was born. Bronze, 18th century, Nepal.

Lest the prediction come true, Suddhodana lavished upon his son a luxurious life. Prince Siddhartha was trained in all the arts and skills expected of a warrior prince. He married Yashodhara, his aunt's daughter, after defeating his cousin Devadatta, another suitor for Yashodhara's hand. Devadatta nursed a grievance against Siddhartha Gautama and made repeated attempts to harm him in the years to come.

Siddhartha nevertheless came face to face with human pain and suffering. His father could not keep his son away from his glorious destiny. While on an outing in the royal parks with his charioteer, Channa, the prince saw three different sights that were to change him and the future of mankind forever. The first sight was of an old man; the second of a diseased man; and the third, of a corpse being followed by weeping mourners. Like the lull after the storm, there was a fourth sight, that of a saint, calm and peaceful.

The Prince Siddhartha sighed. 'Is this', he said, 'That happy earth they brought me forth to see…'

Sir Edwin Arnold **The Light of Asia** 1879

When Kapilavastu rejoiced at the birth of Prince Siddhartha's son, Rahula, Siddhartha did not participate in the festivities. The courtly indulgences aroused aversion in his mind. The magnificent surroundings began to seem like a cemetery filled with dead bodies left to rot. One night, while his wife slept with their newborn son on their nuptial bed, Siddhartha left his home and family with Channa and his favourite horse, Kanthaka.

Far from the city gates of Kapilavastu, he removed his royal regalia and cut off his flowing locks. Kanthaka dropped dead with grief. This is called the Great Renunciation or the Great Going Forth.

Right: Asita and Suddhodana. 2nd century BC, Amravati. National Museum, New Delhi.

Blind is this world; free are they here who clearly see. As birds that escape from a net a few go to a blissful state.

Dhammapada 174

11

The emacipated Buddha who described his futile attempt at self-mortification as time spent trying to tie air into knots.

Even today in Tibetan monasteries, when a novice enters the Order, he is brought bedecked in all his finery for the last time after which he discards them for the robes of the Order.

Having renounced domestic life and the socially oppressive, caste-ridden Brahmanical Hindu religion, the future Buddha began his quest for a release from the endless cycle of birth and death (*samsara*).

For six years Prince Siddhartha roamed as a wandering mendicant, undertaking severe austerities and self-mortification according to the prevalent practices, which left him dark and emaciated. But the knowledge that he was seeking, the path to ending earthly misery and a release from *samsara*, remained elusive.

Just as kusha grass wrongly grasped, cuts the very hand
Even so ascetic life wrongly handled drags one to hell

Dhammapada 311

Above:
Worshipping the Bodhi tree, a constant reminder of the Master's Enlightenment. A panel from Sanchi, 2nd century AD.

In 531 BC, on the banks of the Nairanjana river, near a village called Uruvela, Siddhartha selected a pipal tree (*ficus religiosia*) as the seat for his meditation. The tree was to later become known as the Bodhi or Bo tree.

For 49 days, Gautama sat under the Bodhi tree with single-minded determination. Then piercing the shell of ignorance, he discovered that only by conquering desire could he attain the true path to *Nirvana* (liberation).

Left:
The Buddha unyielding to the temptations of Mara

Faring far, wandering alone, bodiless, lying in a cave, is the mind.
Those who subdue it are free from the bonds of Mara.

Dhammapada 37

13

The Buddha returns to Kapilavastu after seven years and is welcomed by his father, King Suddhodana and his son, Rahula.

The auspicious night when the Lord attained *Nirvana* is, according to Pali tradition, divided into three watches. During the first watch, the future Buddha recalled his earlier lives; in the second, he comprehended the knowledge of death and rebirth of all corporeal beings. In the third watch, he arrived at the three basic components of the *Dharma*, the Four Noble Truths, the Eightfold Path and the Middle Way. With these revelations Siddhartha was freed from rebirth and *samsara*. He became the Perfectly Wise, the *Bhagavat*, the *Arhat*, the *Tathagata*. From then on he was the Buddha or the Enlightened One and entered a living *Nirvana*.

In the Deer Park at Sarnath near Varanasi the
Buddha preached his first sermon,
Dharmachakrapravartana or Turning of the Wheel of
Law, to the five ascetics who had earlier deserted
him. They became his first disciples.

The Four Noble Truths
The world is full of misery and suffering.
Desire and attachment is the root cause of all
misery and suffering.
Cessation of suffering can be achieved by
extinguishing desire.
The path, which leads to the cessation of suffering,
is the Noble Eightfold Path.

The Buddha's doctrine spread rapidly across the towns and cities of the vast Gangetic plains. Ancient Sanskrit and Pali narratives emphasise how the Awakened One drew followers from secular society and from the disciples of other *yogis*. The way in which Buddhism penetrated every strata of society can be illustrated by the story of Yasa, the son of a rich merchant, who woke up one morning to find his luxurious and sensuous life stifling, and he left home despite familial obligations. Convinced by the Enlightened One's teachings on the illusory nature of material success he joined the *Sangha*. Later his father and the rest of his family also followed the path of the Lord and became his first lay disciples.

The simple *mantra* to enter the *Sangha* (the religious community) was the Triple Gems of *Buddha*, *Dharma* and *Sangha*.

Buddham sharanam gachchami
Dharmam sharanam gachchami
Sangham sharanam gachchami

I take refuge in the *Buddha*
I take refuge in the *Dharma*
I take refuge in the *Sangha*

Left: *Dharmachakra* or
Wheel of Law, held up by the lions
– a panel from Sanchi showing the
First Sermon at Sarnath

1 Taxila
2 Mathura
3 Varanasi
4 Sarnath
5 Pataliputra
6 Rajagriha
7 Bodh Gaya
8 Bharhut
9 Sanchi
10 Ajanta
11 Ellora
12 Karle
13 Nagarjuna-
konda
14 Amaravati

A retinue of 1250 monks accompanied the Master on his first visit to Rajir. A large number of followers always accompanied him on his arduous travels to the burgeoning townships of northern India. Monasteries of varying sizes came up in the Ganga valley with patronage from kings and rich merchants. Buddhist egalitarianism kept the doors of the *Sangha* open to everyone.

He who has no conception of I and ME whatsoever towards mind and body, he who grieves not for that which he has not, indeed he is called a Bhikshu.

Dhammapada 367

Pali texts stress the simplicity of the *bhikshu's* life. A typical day in the Buddha's life began with the Master waking up early, meditating and then taking his alms bowl to the nearest town to beg for food. He would be accompanied by other *bhikshus*. After returning, he bathed and had his food before noon. Then after meditating, he received visitors and delivered a sermon. Retiring early in the night, he slept for a few hours, before waking to another identical day. Twentieth century monks still follow this ancient routine set by the Master.

**Below:
The
Dharmachakra,
– a panel from
Sanchi,
2nd century AD**

17

Prajapati Gautami, a queen of the Sakyas, along with 500 women came to the Master at Vaishali, seeking to join the *Sangha*.

To preempt an unfavourable response they had even shaved their heads and donned the orange robes of the monastic order. Other people who took the vows included the Buddha's cousin, Ananda, who later became the Master's favourite attendant, the Buddha's son, Rahula, who was ordained in Kapilavastu at the minimum age of twenty.

Popular events from the Buddha's life. Panel from Nagarjunakonda, 3rd century AD.
National Museum, New Delhi.

Bimbisara, the ruler of Magadha became a follower. His son, Ajatashatru who opposed the Buddha, sent a wild elephant to trample the Master but the compassionate gaze of the Lord tamed the brute. Only then did the mighty King Ajatashatru realise the hollowness of temporal power and joined the righteous path.

Some are tamed by stick, by goads and whips. The elephant was tamed by the great seer without a stick, without a weapon.

Angulimala (literally, one who wears a necklace of fingers), a hardened criminal, underwent a transformation after meeting the Buddha. There is a beautiful legend of a painter engaged by a king, to paint the Master, who found it impossible to concentrate on the Master's serene visage, and could only paint by looking at his reflection in the water.

At Vaishali, the capital of the republican state of the Lichchavis, the Enlightened One met Amrapali, a renowned courtesan. She was so moved by Sakyamuni's teachings on the transient nature of life that she later became a *bhikshuni* or nun.

19

On the banks of the Hiranyavati in Kushinagar, where the Lord left his mortal body.
Inset: Worshipping the stupa which reverentially encases the remains of the Lord – a panel from Sanchi.

At the age of 80, in 486 BC, the Buddha spent his last rainy season at a village near Vaishali. The Master's last meal was a gift from the metalsmith, Chunda, who had prepared a dish of *sukkara maddava* (variously identified as wild mushrooms and pork) for the *Sangha*. Perceiving danger in the food after eating it, the Buddha asked Chunda to bury the rest and not to serve it to the others. He insisted that Chunda feel no remorse, for one who has served the Buddha his last meal would gain great merit. In spite of being severely ill, the Lord insisted on moving with the *Sangha* to the small town of Kushinagar.

Below: Elephants carrying the Master's relics. Bharhut, 2nd century BC. National Museum, New Delhi.

The Buddha asked his followers to visit the four places associated with his life - Lumbini, where he was born, Bodh Gaya, where he attained Enlightenment, Sarnath, where he preached his First Sermon and Kushinagar, the site of his *Mahaparinirvana*.

On the auspicious full moon day of *Vaisakha*,
the same day that this earth had been blessed
with his Birth and the same day on which he
had attained *Nirvana*, the Lord attained
Mahaparinirvana.

From attachment springs grief,
From attachment springs fear;
For him who is wholly free from attachment there is no grief,
Hence where is fear?

From lust springs grief,
From lust springs fear;
For him who is wholly free from lust there is no grief,
Hence where is fear?

From craving springs grief,
From craving springs fear;
For him who is wholly free from craving there is no grief,
Hence where is fear?

Dhammapada 211-13

SPREAD OF THE DHARMA

O Bhikshus! There are two extremes that should be avoided by a recluse. Indulgence in sensual pleasures - this is base, vulgar, worldly, ignoble and profitless; and addiction to self-mortification - this is painful, ignoble and profitless.

Abandoning both these extremes the Tathagata has comprehended the Middle Path which promotes sight and knowledge and tends to peace, higher wisdom, enlightenment and Nirvana.

Thus spoke the Buddha at Sarnath in his first sermon, the *Dharmachakrapravartana* or Turning of the Wheel of Law, which put forth the Middle Way, the Four Noble Truths and the Eightfold Path.

The Wheel – the eternal signifier of the Dharma. A panel from the great stupa at Sanchi.

The message of the Buddha spread rapidly, penetrating caste and class barriers. The Buddha preached that the way to salvation was not dependent on God or Divine Grace but on understanding the way things really are. It is essentially concerned with man, or rather with all living, suffering beings caught in the treadmill of desire and craving.

23

Sakyamuni's message encapsulated complex issues of existence in a lucid manner, punctuated with anecdotes from day-to-day life:

One day the Buddha encountered a woman who begged the Lord to save her dead child. The Lord asked the woman to get a mustard seed from a household that had not experienced death. The woman came back after a while, unsuccessful but sobered, and fell at the feet of the Master. The Buddha then expounded to her the transitory nature of human existence.

Rock-cut statue of the Buddha from Avukana, Sri Lanka, 9th century.

By the time the Buddha attained *Mahaparinirvana* (final extinction) at the age of 80 years, the teachings he had propounded had a large following in north India, especially among the warrior and the merchant classes. Buddhism's appeal lay in its vision of a world where deliverance from the caste-ridden and ritualistic Brahmanical Hindu order was possible. Above all, the Enlightened One preached that salvation was in one's own hands, possible in this world, by freeing oneself from desire.

Empty this boat, O Bhikshu! Emptied by you it will move swiftly. Cutting out lust and hatred, to Nirvana you will thereby go.

Dhammapada 369

A rich tapestry of colour amidst resplendent life size Buddha statues and paintings. Dambulla, Sri Lanka.

A few months after the *Mahaparinirvana*, a great gathering of monks, popularly known as the First Buddhist Council, took place at Saptaparni caves near Rajagriha. The teachings of the Master were codified for the first time and the *Vinaya Pitaka* and the *Sutra Pitaka* were compiled. A Second Buddhist Council was held at Vaishali a hundred years later where schisms arose regarding points of monastic discipline and philosophy between the orthodox Sthaviravadins (elders) and the Mahasanghikas (the great community). The Third Council at Pataliputra was held under the patronage of the Mauryan emperor, Ashoka. His son, Mahendra, and daughter, Sanghamitra, went to Sri Lanka to spread the teachings of the Great Master there.

A cutting of the sacred Bodhi tree being brought to Sri Lanka. 19th century mural.

Emperor Ashoka whose reign spanned from 268 to 239 BC, converted to Buddhism after he experienced a crisis of conscience following his bloody victory at the Kalinga war where he was responsible for the ruthless massacre of tens and thousands of innocent victims.

After embracing the Faith in 260 BC, Ashoka attempted to rule by the *Dharma*, justice and non-violence associated with Buddha's teachings. Ashoka took major steps to popularise Buddhism throughout his vast empire.

As early as in the first hundred years after the Lord's *Mahaparinirvana*, different schools of thought arose within Buddhism. This was a result of the intense debates within the monastic order. The influence of rituals and the devotional philosophy that pervaded Hinduism was also a factor. The most significant result was the rise of the Mahayana (meaning great vehicle), while the older school was called Hinayana (meaning little vehicle).

Mahayana doctrine represented a great ferryboat that would take humanity across the sea of suffering and rebirth to the shore of *Nirvana*. The Mahayana school shifted the focus from *Arhat* to *Boddhisattva*. The Boddhisattva was one who postponed his entry into *Nirvana* until he could lead all other beings to *Nirvana* as well, it laid emphasis on salvation for all. This was a departure from the ideal of the earlier school where the *Arhat* was the person seeking *Nirvana* for his personal salvation. To the Mahayana school, the Buddha was not only a teacher but also a saviour.

In Sri Lanka, the school of the elders held its own against the Mahayana tide and was known as the Theravada. Under the patronage of powerful kings like Parakkramabahu (1153-86), Sinhalese monks took Theravada to Burma. The *Dharma* was established in Thailand a century later, while Cambodia and Laos adopted Buddhism in the 14th century.

From the famed *mahaviharas* (monastic universities) of north India, Buddhism went

Right :
Bhutanese Temple, Bodh Gaya.

Below:
Prayers for peace - outside the Vishwa Shanti Stupa in Rajgir.

to China by way of traders as early as 50 BC and from there to Korea. Buddhism went to Japan from Korea in the 6th century AD.

Zen Buddhism was introduced in Japan in the mid-12th century but its strict stipulations and subtleties, with emphasis on personal effort, did not attract many followers in the beginning.

The crux of Zen philosophy is the Mahayana theory of universal Buddhahood. Zen is Japanese for Chinese *Ch'an*, which is derived from Sanskrit *dhyana* (meditation).

27

Atisha, the great saint who propagated the Dharma in the Land of Snows, Tibet.

In the 8th century AD Santarakshita from Nalanda Mahavihara went to Tibet to spread Buddhism. Facing hostilities from the local populace, he was forced to return. Soon after, Acharya Padmasambhava, the great Buddhist Tantric Master from Kashmir, was able to successfully establish Buddhism in Tibet. Tibetan Buddhists revere him as Guru Rinpoche.

Right: Preaching Buddha statue in clay. A typical example of the confluence of styles from the Silk Route – Dunhuang caves, 7th century AD, China.

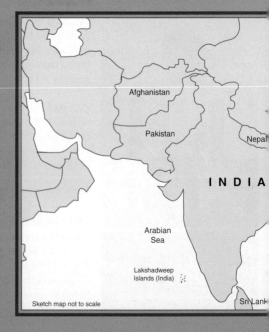

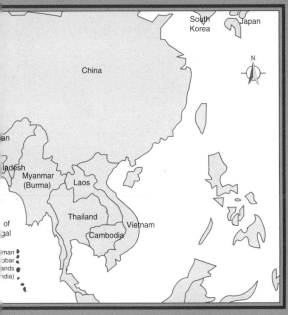

Left:
Maitreya,
the future
Buddha.
Tashilunpo
Monastery,
Tibet.

A new school of Buddhism, Vajrayana (*vajra* meaning thunderbolt) arose in Tibet around the 8th century. It is often described as the 'completed *Dharma*', because it absorbed the doctrines of both Theravada and Mahayana and also embraced *tantra*.

From Tibet, Buddhism spread to Mongolia and the rugged Mongols were converted to one of the gentlest faiths ever propagated. The genius of Buddhism was that local specificities were taken into account and thus Buddhist *Dharma* became thoroughly integrated into the culture of each country, from the islands of Japan to the landlocked mountains of Tibet and Mongolia.

In the Bhutanese Temple, Bodh Gaya.
The bright alternating colours with clouds and sceneries are typical of the Tibetan style.

The resurgence of devotional Hinduism, incorporating popular cults and Buddhist practices like *ahimsa, puja* worship and vegetarianism, narrowed the differences between Hinduism and Buddhism in everyday life. The Turkish invasions beginning in the 10th century dealt a further blow to Buddhism in India and the major monasteries of India were wiped off the map. Thereafter, Buddhism has never come back as a major force in the land of Sakyamuni's birth.

In modern India, Buddhism survives only in isolated pockets among the peoples of Ladakh, Lahaul, Spiti, Kinnaur in the western Himalayas and the Monpas, Sherdukpens, Lepchas, Bhutias and Chakmas in the eastern Himalayas. The conversion of some sections of depressed class Hindus under the leadership of Dr B R Ambedkar in the late 1950s and 1960s is an instance of Buddhist revival in India.

The flight of His Holiness the XIVth Dalai Lama from Tibet in 1959, following Chinese persecution, led to the establishment of his government-in-exile in Dharamsala in north India, where there is a thriving Tibetan Buddhist community. The Tibetan influence has led to the founding of more than a hundred monasteries all over India, besides reviving older ones, especially in the western Himalayas.

The tall spires of the Mahabodhi Temple in Bodh Gaya, a tribute to the supreme moment in the Master's life when he achieved *Nirvana*.

Europe was initiated into Buddhist philosophy with early 19th century colonial administrators, linguists and scholars taking active interest in the ancient texts of the Orient. The works of Col Henry Olcott, the American co-founder of Theosophical Society, and Edwin Arnold's poem, *The Light of Asia*, published in 1879, further spurred this intellectual curiosity. However, it was not till the middle of this century that Buddhism as a religion espousing non-violence was firmly entrenched in the consciousness of post-War Europe. Travellers who had been to the East returned to Europe and North America immersed in Buddhist philosophy. Asian teachers arrived in Europe, often on teaching visits. Some of them established Buddhist centres with communities of monks and lay people living under the guidance of *Dharma* masters.

Mural at Tabo Monastery, 11th century.

IMAGES FOR POSTERITY

Art & Architecture

Art as the sacred expression of religion is best exemplified in Buddhist art and architecture. The aesthetic expression of this art and architecture can be witnessed throughout the great expanse of the Asian landmass.

The beginnings were however very modest with the Master asking his followers to undertake a retreat (*vassavasa*) during the rainy season lest they trample the newly sprouted vegetation. From these early temporary residences, the thatched huts, caverns and caves hewn out of rocks, arose the *vihara*.

After the Master's *Mahaparinirvana*, his body was cremated and the ashes divided into eight portions. Thereafter the ashes, duly enshrined in caskets, were placed in *stupas* where they were venerated as in the Hindu burial mounds of the times. Stupas were built all over India as they symbolised the Master's *Nirvana*. In Tibetan, the stupas are called *chorten* and remains of great *lamas* are encased here.

Emperor Ashoka fostered the existing tradition of erecting pillars, giving it an unrivalled technical finesse, exemplified by the polish that has remained undiminished to this day. The pillars were adorned with animal capitals like the lion capital at Sarnath. This has been adopted as the state emblem of independent India in 1947.

Ashoka erected pillars in all corners of the empire, proclaiming the *Dharma* in the language of the people, Prakrit, using the Brahmi script. In the northwest provinces the script was Kharosti and in the Gandhara region in the extreme northwest it was in Aramaic and Greek.

Early stupas like the one at Sanchi were situated on the trade routes and were constantly being enlarged due to mercantile munificence reflected in the four *toranas* or gateways situated at the four corners.

Each *torana* has three richly embellished architraves which end in volutes. They resemble a picture scroll or *pata citra*,

which was employed by storytellers, bards and teachers to recount the tales of yore, the Jataka tales being the favourite subject. Sanchi, Bharhut and Amravati represent a continuum, culminating in the stupa at Amravati. Chaityas, the Bodhi tree and the throne were also favourite motifs.

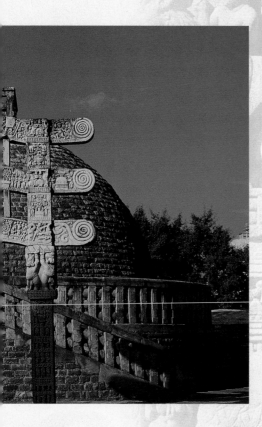

Emperor Ashoka is said to have built 84,000 stupas and renovated many more, of which the Sanchi stupa is the best known.

The *anda* or the hemispherical dome was the main body, which symbolised the cosmic mountain, with later stupas becoming increasingly cylindrical. Three circular discs on top of the *anda* were called the *chattraveli* or umbrella, a traditional honorific and auspicious symbol, standing for the *Triratna* or Three Jewels of Buddhism (the *Buddha*, the *Dharma* and the *Sangha*).

Nalanda in Bihar has the ruins of one
of the world's oldest universities,
founded in the 5th century AD. In the
7th century Hiuen Tsang spent twelve
years, both as a student and a teacher,
at Nalanda which once had over 3,000
teachers and philosophers, attracting
students from countries as far flung
as Java, Sumatra, Korea, Japan
and China.

**Above:
Bodhisattvas,
Nalanda, 5th-6th
century AD.**

**Right: Marble
stupa, relief from
Amaravati, 2nd
century AD.**

The imposing chaitya at Karle in Maharashtra. Early 2nd century AD.

Huge rock-cut *chaityas* (halls of worship) and viharas for the monks were carved in the hills far away from major towns but close to the trade routes. Many chaityas are found in Maharashtra, at Bhaja, Bedsa, Nasik and Karle and in Bihar, the Lomas Rishi chaitya at Barabar hills.

Gandhara
Buddha,
1st century AD.
National
Museum,
New Delhi.

In the early phases of Buddhist art, the Buddha was symbolically depicted by showing a pair of footprints or an empty throne. In Mahayana tradition, the Buddha was deified and viewed as a saviour. During the reign of the great Kushan emperor, Kanishka (about 78 AD), the Mathura school of art started the tradition of transforming Buddha's symbols into human form to facilitate worship.

In the Mathura region during the Kushan period, the traditional figure of the Buddha as the meditative *yogin* was carved for the first time, keeping the *yaksha* prototype in mind. The *yakshas* and other spirits were worshipped before the time of the Buddha. The early images of the Buddha were massive forms rendered in rough, unpolished sandstone with broad shoulders. The Buddha was portrayed with special attributes or *lakshanas* which were the marks of great beings. Of the 32 *lakshanas* on the Buddha's person the *urna* or tuft of hair on the forehead, *ushnisha* or cranial protuberance, symbols of the wheel on the soles of the feet, were carved.

The Buddha in the *Bhumisparsha mudra*. 13th century, Nepal. An example of the unparalleled skills of the Newari artisans who continue the tradition of metal-casting Buddha images.

At the same time, in the northwestern region of Gandhara, there emerged a different school of art which reflected Greek influence. The most striking characteristics of Gandhara art was that Buddha was robed in the toga, a typically European garment, and his facial features were quite Hellenistic.

The Gupta period (4th - 7th century AD) saw Sarnath emerging as a school par excellence in Buddhist art. One of the best examples of this period is the preaching Buddha in the *dharmachakrapravartana mudra*, which is now at Sarnath Museum.

There is a belief, which persists even today, that to commission an image of the Buddha would earn spiritual merit.

The Buddhist religion, despite having a founder who had not supported the making of images and preached a doctrine against material possessions, acquired the world's richest and most varied system of visual support.

Buddhist iconography followed the Indian cultural tradition of using elaborate hand gestures (*mudras*) to depict a wide range of moods and emotions. The above panel from Pala period, 10th century, illustrates the following *mudras*, from left to right:

Sarana Palm facing the devotee, implying protection in the path of the Dharma.

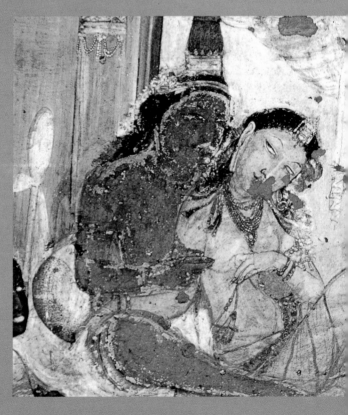

Bhumisparsha (also fourth from left)
The Buddha calls on the earth as a witness to
his Enlightenment

Dharmachakrapravartana The Buddha turns
the Wheel of Law

Dhyani Arms clasped, the right above the left,
signifying meditation

Beginning with the 2nd century BC and continuing into the 6th century AD, the paintings, and to a lesser known degree, the sculptures in the caves of Ajanta inspired by Buddhism and its compassionate ethos, unleashed a surge of artistic excellence unmatched in human history. The creative use of colour and freedom of expression used in depicting human and animal forms makes the cave paintings at Ajanta one of the high watermarks of artistic creativity. The nearby cave complex of Ellora, though not exclusively Buddhist, continued to foster the artistic legacy of Ajanta for a couple of more centuries.

Painting from Ajanta Caves.

Perched precariously on craggy cliffs and snow-capped mountains of the Himalayan range, the box-shaped gompas (monasteries) break the monotony of the treeless landscape in Ladakh. Alchi and Thikse in Ladakh are storehouses of *tangkhas* and richly painted clay images of the Buddha. *Tangkhas* are mainly used for worship. *Tangkhas* also serve as a visual aid to meditation. *Tangkhas* are also put up in houses to ward off the evil eye and act as a good luck charm.

Giant cloth banners (*snon-grol*) are often unfurled on the slopes of mountains during the annual monastic festivals when the *cham* dances take place. The most commonly used images on the *tangkhas* range from the Buddha, Bodhisattvas, Taras, esoteric tutelary deities and *mandalas*, each serving a

specific purpose. The Buddhas, Bodhisattvas and Taras are painted in light colours whereas the tutelary deities are painted in dark and sharply alternating colours providing a contrast.

Mandala. 15th-16th century, Tibet. Tantric ideas were initiated by lay devotees, who sought through chants, ritual gestures and *mandalas*, the power that would transform them into siddhas or yogis.

45

The Master's words of
wisdom being preserved
for posterity. Mural
from Dunhuang caves,
Gansu province, China.

Left:
Inscribed in gold,
front page from the
Tengyur, a 225 volume
Tibetan religious text.

Right:
The words of the
Dharma - chiselled on
stone to withstand the
ravages of time.

PAGES OF WISDOM

Literature

In monasteries perched on hillsides in the arid moonscape of Ladakh and among emerald rice fields in Thailand, young saffron clad monks sway and recite the same prayers. The Buddha's teachings are inscribed on prayer wheels in Mongolia, *tangkha* paintings in Tibet and palm leaf manuscripts in Sri Lanka. After 2500 years, Gautama Buddha still lives in his teachings which have not been forgotten.

After the *Mahaparinirvana* of the Buddha at Kushinagar, the legends and myths, the commentaries and analyses began. Buddhist literature began with what the Buddha said and around it a body of canonical and non-canonical writing emerged. The earliest Buddhist literature to have survived is in Pali.

The oldest Buddhist canonical writings like the *Vinaya* and *Sutra Pitakas* began as oral literature. Buddhist tradition has it that at the First Great Council of monks at Rajgir after the death of the Master, his two disciples recited his teachings from memory. Upali recalled the *Vinaya Pitaka* and Ananda the *Sutra Pitaka*.

The earliest Pali canon, the *Tripitaka*, consists of three anthologies of writings, *Vinaya*, *Sutra* and *Abhidharma Pitakas*. It is an immense body of writing, with each *Pitaka* divided into a number of books and further subdivided into commentaries and abstracts.

Vinaya Pitaka, the Book of Discipline, deals with the rules of monastic order, while *Sutra Pitaka*, the Book of Discourses, deals with the ethical principles of the Buddha's teachings. *Abhidharma Pitaka*, a collection on abstract philosophy, elaborates on the metaphysical principles underlying the doctrine.

Dhammapada, or In the Steps of the *Dharma*, is a book people instantly connect with the sermons of Gautama Buddha. Its terse sayings are in Pali verse, on a variety of subjects ranging from happiness, anger and craving to Enlightenment. These verses, memorised by young monks and lay believers of all ages across the world, embody the very spirit of the Buddha's teachings.

Above: A cosmos in miniature, the Yantra, a sacred diagram used by the Tantra school as an aid to meditation.

In the verses of the *Theragatha* and *Therigatha* one can still hear the poetic voices of *bhikshus* and *bhikshunis* describing how their lives were transformed by the teachings of the Buddha. Many of the poets were contemporaries of Sakyamuni. The verses by the *bhikshus* in the *Theragatha* are often spiritual and meditative, with many beautiful passages on nature while the nuns strike a more personal note and sing to the joys, sorrows and complexities of life. The *Therigatha* is the earliest anthology of women's writing in India, and includes verses by Amrapali, the courtesan of Vaishali who became a *bhikshuni*.

Though I am weak and tired now,
And my youthful step long gone,
Leaning on this staff, I climb the mountain peak....
And over my spirit blows the breath of liberty
I have won, I have won the triple gems.
The Buddha's way is mine.

Mettika **Therigatha** 5th century BC

Below: Two ancient centres of learning, Dharmarajika Stupa in Taxila (right) and Nalanda Mahavihara (left).

A *bhikshu* explaining to novices the teachings of the Master.

Children across the Buddhist world grow up listening to the Jataka tales. Jataka means 'birth stories' and they chronicle the former incarnations of the Buddha as a man and as an animal. The stories have been told and retold for centuries to popularise the teachings of the Master. More than 500 stories still exist, many of them with animals as the main characters and have the humour and liveliness of folk tales and fables.

Narrative in stone - a panel illustrating a Jataka tale, Ikshavaku period, Andhra Pradesh. National Museum, New Delhi.

Though many of the Jataka stories have a moral, some are simple adventure tales. At the end of each story the hero is identified as a Bodhisattva. Episodes from the tales are carved on the gateways of the stupas of Sanchi and Bharhut among other sites, and also painted in the Ajanta Caves.

THE LION AND THE JACKAL

One day Ananda was given 500 pieces of cloth and he distributed them among the brothers. The king who had given them asked why he had done so. Ananda replied that this was the custom of the Sangha. The king gave him 500 more. At that time Ananda was assisted by another bhikshu who did him many services and he gave the second bundle of cloths to this bhikshu, who distributed them. Some monks complained to the Buddha about Ananda giving all the pieces of cloth to one particular bhikshu. The Buddha explained that as the bhikshu had earlier helped Ananda, one good turn deserved another and that gratitude is a sound virtue. The Lord then told the story…

Once a lion lived in the mountain. The mountain was surrounded by water but near the foot there was an island of marshy grass-covered land. One day while hunting, the lion was caught in this mud and stayed for seven days without food. On the seventh day a jackal saw him and ran away terrified but returned on hearing the pleas of the lion. The jackal made a channel of water that softened the mud, then he got beneath the body of the lion and freed him.

The lion killed a bull and in gratitude offered the jackal the first share of the kill before eating it himself. Taking some food for their wives they headed home. The lion invited the jackal and his wife to his own cave. He told them that they could live in the small cave at the entrance of his cave and promised to care for them.

The families lived happily together and the young lion cubs played with the young jackals. After a while the lioness began to resent the attention the lion paid to the jackal. She hinted to the jackals that they should leave.

While hunting together, the jackal mentioned this to the lion. The lion was amazed and said he did not want the jackals to leave. Reaching home, the lion reminded his wife of the time when for seven days he was caught in the mud and the way the jackal had saved him. Finally the lioness understood and from then the two families lived in harmony.

"A friend who plays a friendly part, however small and weak he be, He is my kinsman and my flesh and blood, a friend and comrade he; Despise him not, my sharp-fanged mate! This jackal saved my life for me."

Then the Buddha identified the birth: Ananda was the jackal, "I myself was the lion."

One of the most interesting non-canonical work is *Milindapanha* or Questions of Milinda, which was written in Sanskrit in India in the beginning of the Christian era. The book is a dialogue between Milinda (Menander), a Greco-Bactrian king of Sakala (modern Sialkot in Pakistan) and a Buddhist monk, Nagasena. Milinda begins as a doubting man but by the end he is converted by Nagasena's brilliant replies and becomes an ardent believer.

The XIVth Dalai Lama preaching in Bodh Gaya.

The most famous life stories of the Buddha are *Lalitavistara* of the Sarvastivadin sect and *Buddhacharita* composed by the poet Aswaghosha in the 1st century AD. Then there are the three great Sri Lankan verse chronicles - *Dipavamsa*, the Island Chronicle; the *Mahavamsa*, the Great Chronicle; and *Culavamsa*, the Lesser Chronicle. These are works in progress with monks constantly adding to them. They narrate the history of Buddhism in Sri Lanka.

Reverentially draped with colourful silk, the religious texts at the library of Lamayuru Monastery in Ladakh.

Buddhist literature is a gift to the world from thousands of forgotten monks and nuns who preserved the manuscripts in their monasteries with care and devotion. In their fragile pages we can still hear the wise, compassionate voice of one of the greatest thinkers of world civilisation.

OM MANI PADME HUM
The sacred mantra in Tibetan, engraved on rocks and pebbles by devotees.

SACRED SITES

In one of his last utterances before his *Mahaparinirvana*, the Buddha said to Ananda, his favourite attendant.

There are these four places, Ananda, which the believing man should visit with feelings of reverence and awe.

Which are the four?

The place, Ananda, at which the believing man can say, 'Here the Tathagata was born'

The place, Ananda, at which the believing man can say, 'Here the Tathagata attained to the supreme and perfect insight'.

The place, Ananda, at which the believing man can say, 'Here was the kingdom of righteousness set on foot by the Tathagata'.

The place, Ananda, at which the believing man can say, 'Here the Tathagata passed finally away in that utter passing away which leaves nothing whatever to remain behind'.

Mahaparinirvana Sutra (The Book of the Great Decease), Chapter V

BIHAR

● Major cities

● Sacred sites

In the following section, **Sacred Sites**, the four places mentioned by Gautama Buddha: Lumbini, Bodh Gaya, Sarnath and Kushinagar, which constitute the *Dharma Yatra*, are described with reference to their past as well as to the present.

Included in this section are chapters on Rajgir, Sravasti and Vaishali; places which are associated with the life of the Buddha. There is also a chapter on Nalanda, the site of the famous Buddhist monastery, 11 kms from Rajgir. These eight chapters have been sequentially arranged, starting with Lumbini, the place of the Buddha's birth, and closing with Kushinagar, where, at the age of eighty, he left his earthly body and attained *Mahaparinirvana*. However, it is not advisable to visit the sacred sites in the sequential order in which they have been arranged in the book, as practical reasons necessitate otherwise.

From the point of entry into India at one of the four metros, Delhi, Calcutta, Chennai (Madras) or Mumbai (Bombay), it is best for the visitor to travel to either Patna in Bihar or Varanasi in Uttar Pradesh.

Buddhist Pilgrimages

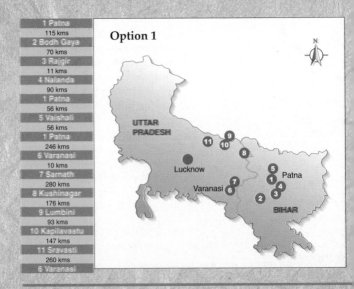

1 Patna
115 kms
2 Bodh Gaya
70 kms
3 Rajgir
11 kms
4 Nalanda
90 kms
1 Patna
56 kms
5 Vaishali
56 kms
1 Patna
246 kms
6 Varanasi
10 kms
7 Sarnath
280 kms
8 Kushinagar
176 kms
9 Lumbini
93 kms
10 Kapilavastu
147 kms
11 Sravasti
260 kms
6 Varanasi

Option 1

They are both well connected by air and rail to all the metros and make ideal gateways for visiting the sacred sites. Patna and Varanasi, the ancient Indian towns of Pataliputra and Kashi were also thriving townships during the Buddha's lifetime. Keeping this in mind, the next two chapters are on Patna and Varanasi.

In later sections in this book, **Practical Information** and **Travellers Needs**, factual information that will be needed by visitors, pilgrims as well as tourists, to these sites are provided. The former gives information required by visitors arriving in India, at Delhi, Calcutta, Chennai or Mumbai. **Travellers Needs** details factual information on Patna, Varanasi and the eight sacred sites.

To facilitate travel in this holy land sanctified by the Buddha's footsteps long centuries ago, we have listed the following itineraries which would be useful for the pilgrim. However, these routes are not necessarily the only options available to the pilgrim, and the sacred sites could be visited in any order preferred by the visitor.

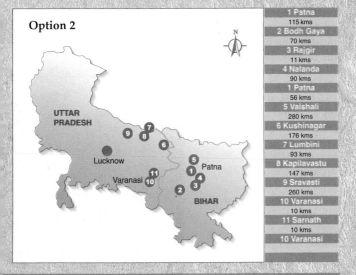

Option 2

1 Patna	
	115 kms
2 Bodh Gaya	
	70 kms
3 Rajgir	
	11 kms
4 Nalanda	
	90 kms
1 Patna	
	56 kms
5 Vaishali	
	280 kms
6 Kushinagar	
	176 kms
7 Lumbini	
	93 kms
8 Kapilavastu	
	147 kms
9 Sravasti	
	260 kms
10 Varanasi	
	10 kms
11 Sarnath	
	10 kms
10 Varanasi	

Patna
BIHAR

Patna, the state capital of Bihar, situated on the banks of the Ganga, is a major entry point for pilgrims wishing to travel in the footsteps of the Buddha. Patna (ancient Pataligram, Pataliputra) is well connected by air, rail and road to Calcutta, Delhi, Mumbai and Varanasi.

Bihar derives its name from *vihara*, meaning Buddhist monastery, as there were once a number of Buddhist monasteries in Bihar. Bodh Gaya, Rajgir and Nalanda in the south, and Vaishali in the north, formed a significant part of the *Buddhakshetra* or the domain of the Great Master's spiritual pursuits.

As the Lord traversed the dusty plains, spreading his message, he had to cross the mighty river Ganga and a small town that stood on its banks, Pataligram. It commanded the river traffic providing endless trade opportunities. The Magadha monarchs decided to move their capital here, from neighbouring Rajgir in the 6th century BC. King Ajatashatru started building a fort here which the Buddha saw in his last days and he made a

prophecy – that of all the famous places, busy marts and centres of commerce, Pataligram will be the greatest, but three dangers will threaten it always – fire, flood and feud. It holds true even today.

The humble Pataligram blossomed into Pataliputra, the mighty capital of the Magadha Empire. From the 6th century BC to the 4th century AD, under the two major dynasties, the Mauryas and the Guptas, Pataliputra reached its zenith. Foreign emissaries like Megasthenes from Greece and Chinese scholar pilgrims like Fa Hien, recount the architectural grandeur and material prosperity of this great city.

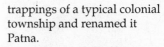

What brought far more enduring renown to Pataliputra and to the Mauryan Empire was Emperor Ashoka (260 BC - 239 BC) who spread the Master's message of peace and non-violence, compassion and love, far and wide. The Third Buddhist Council was held in Pataliputra under his patronage.

A massive flood in the river Sonebhadra in the latter half of the 6th century AD and subsequent Hun invasions devastated the city. In the 16th century, under the Afghan king, Sher Shah Suri, it partly regained its lost glory. In the 19th century it came under the political suzerainty of the British who gave it the trappings of a typical colonial township and renamed it Patna.

Modern Patna is a densely populated, ever-expanding metropolis stretching for over 15 kms, along the south banks of the Ganga. The sprawling ground called Gandhi Maidan forms the hub of this city. Most of the shopping complexes, hotels, offices, schools, colleges and hospitals are located in this area.

Nothing much remains of its glorious past except the ruins of Pataliputra that can be seen in Kumrahar about 6 kms from Gandhi Maidan. The remains of a massive assembly hall with bases of 80 pillars have been excavated at the site, of which only one pillar remains intact. Fa Hien who came here in the 5th century AD found the pillars shining bright as glass.

Patna Museum, established by the British in I917, houses more than 50,000 rare and valuable antiquities and art objects. The most prized possession here is the Holy Relic Casket containing the sacred ashes of the Buddha, unearthed in Vaishali.

A crowned Buddha with Bodhisattvas, 9th century, eastern India, Patna Museum.

Of special interest in Patna Museum are the extensive sections on stone sculptures on the ground floor, especially the Buddha and Bodhisattva figures, and narrative panels in blue schist stone of the Gandhara school. Among the best pieces found here are the black basalt stone figures of Avalokiteshwara, Maitreya and the Buddha discovered at the Vishnupur in Gaya District.

Less than half a kilometre from Gandhi Maidan is Golghar, a mammoth concrete granary built by the British, subsequent to the great famine of 1770. Two spiral staircases from either side lead to the top, which affords a panoramic view of the Ganga and the town.

At Chimni Ghat stands the Patthar ki Masjid, built in 1621 by Parwez Shah, a son of the Mughal emperor, Jahangir, when he was the governor of Bihar.

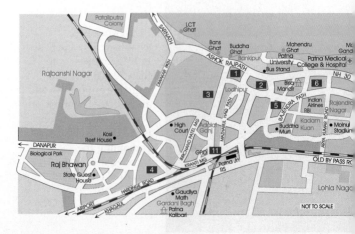

Golghar, the great granary, inaugurated in 1786 for the perpetual prevention of famine!

Gurudwara Har Mandir Sahib, popularly known as Patna Sahib, the sacred shrine of the Sikhs, is 11 kms from the Gandhi Maidan. The site is hallowed as the birthplace of the 10th Guru of the Sikhs, Guru Gobind Singh.

Across the road is the Jalan Museum which stands on the site of Sher Shah's fort and today houses a private art collection. It can be visited only with prior permission. Between Patna and Patna Sahib is Gulzarbagh, where the opium factory and the storehouses of the British were located. It now houses the Government Printing Press.

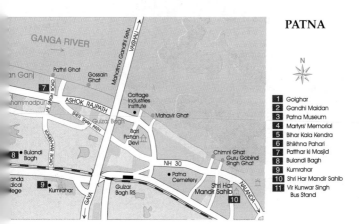

PATNA

1 Golghar
2 Gandhi Maidan
3 Patna Museum
4 Martyrs' Memorial
5 Bihar Kala Kendra
6 Bhikhna Pahari
7 Patthar ki Masjid
8 Bulandi Bagh
9 Kumrahar
10 Shri Har Mandir Sahib
11 Vir Kunwar Singh Bus Stand

UTTAR
PRADESH

Varanasi

Varanasi stands on the west bank of the river Ganga as it flows through the north Indian state of Uttar Pradesh. It is at a distance of 764 kms from Delhi, 678 kms from Calcutta, and Kathmandu, the capital of Nepal is a 12 hour drive away. Varanasi is connected by good metalled roads to the pilgrim sites of Sarnath which is only 10 kms away, as well as to Lumbini, Kapilavastu, Kushinagar and Sravasti.

Over twentyfive centuries ago, a sage travelled 200 kms from Bodh Gaya, where he had attained *Nirvana*, to reach the *ghats* of Varanasi or Kashi as it was then called. The city had seen saffron clad spiritual teachers before him, who came here, drawn by its magnetic, inexplicable spiritual power. The sage was looking for five Hindu ascetics, old companions from whom he had parted, because they had insisted that the only path to salvation was through self-mortification. The Buddha found them at Rishipattana, the Deer Park near Kashi, and gave them the gift of the spiritual knowledge which he had attained since he parted with them, and they became his first followers, and the first members of the *Sangha*.

VARANASI

A time would come when the Buddha's teachings would travel to lands he had never seen, his image worshipped in temples and his name chanted in monasteries. However for Kashi, that summer two thousand five hundred years ago, he was just another pilgrim.

Varanasi, Benares, Kashi, they have called this city by many names. Placed between the Varuna and the Assi rivers it is Varanasi. It is the spiritual pilgrimage that is like a luminous beacon to Hindus and for them it has always been Kashi, the city of light. They believe bathing in the river Ganga here washes away their sins. It is also Avimukta, the city that is never forsaken by Lord Shiva, its ruling deity. It is Shiva's favourite city, his Anandavana or Garden of Bliss. And finally, it is also the *Mahashmashana*, the great cremation ground.

Living with the great questions of birth and death, Varanasi has never bothered to record its history. Its beginnings are lost in the mists of time, no one cares to remember when this city began. It was there when Jerusalem, Beijing and Athens rose and it has watched great cities like Nineveh and Babylon get swallowed by the sand. It is one of the oldest living cities in the world.

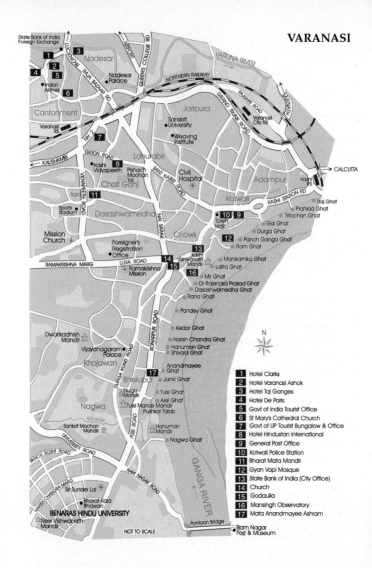

State Bank of India
Foreign Exchange

1 Hotel Clarks
2 Hotel Varanasi Ashok
3 Hotel Taj Ganges
4 Hotel De Paris
5 Govt of India Tourist Office
6 St Mary's Cathedral Church
7 Govt of UP Tourist Bungalow & Office
8 Hotel Hindustan International
9 General Post Office
10 Kotwali Police Station
11 Bharat Mata Mandir
12 Gyan Vapi Mosque
13 State Bank of India (City Office)
14 Church
15 Godaulia
16 Mansingh Observatory
17 Mata Anandmayee Ashram

The best introduction to
Varanasi is from the river. The
city stands by a curve of the
Ganga river, with the stone
steps of the numerous *ghats*
sweeping down to the water.
At dawn, hire a boat and drift
past the *ghats* and the city will
float past like a hand operated
bioscope. Begin from
Dasashwamedha, one of the
holiest *ghats*, where the gods
are said to have performed
the ten-horse sacrifice. The
river will be thronged with

early-morning bathers
standing chest deep in the
water as they raise their faces
to the rising sun and recite the
sacred *mantra*. One can see the
perpetual movement of the
pilgrims on the steps, the vivid
colours of their clothes
glistening against the pale
gold water, the triangular flags
fluttering atop the temple
spires.

The panorama of the *ghats* is
one of the most arresting

images of Varanasi. As you float down the river some will be crowded with bathers, at others a solitary, ash-smeared *sadhu* with matted hair will be communing with the sun. Another *ghat* will be full of washermen slapping clothes on flat stones in a synchronised swinging of arms.

A blue grey haze of drifting smoke covers the most fascinating *ghat* of all, Manikarnika. Only those fortunate to have died in Varanasi have the privilege to be cremated here. To die here is to be freed from the cycle of life and death. And with the city's usual penchant for myth making they named this ghat *manikarnika*, after the goddess Parvati's earring which fell down while bathing. On top of the steps is a large tank, the Manikarnika Kund that Lord Vishnu is supposed to have dug with his *chakra* and filled with his perspiration. Vishnu's feet are set in a marble pedestal beside it, called the Charanapaduka.

At the heart of this city is the Kashi Vishwanath Temple, the holiest shrine of Lord Shiva. Here he is also called Vishweshwara, the lord of the world and the city is said to sit atop his *trishul* (trident).

The old localities of Varanasi are a labyrinth of narrow lanes called *galis*, crowded with people, cycles, and ambling cows. Some of them are so narrow even a cycle rickshaw cannot pass through. The streetcorner food shops make trays of sweets, the famous creamy *rabri* or thickened milk and glasses of cool *thandai* and *lassi*. And the *paan* shops offer a variety of *paans* (betel leaves) with a subtle mix of *masala*. You have to walk down the narrow Vishwanath Gali to the temple. It is a serpentine alley lined with shops selling brass and trinkets, silks and flower garlands and crowded with pilgrims. A Shiva Temple has stood here for 1500 hundred years but the present temple is not an old one because over the centuries it has been destroyed many times by Muslim invaders. The Mughal Emperor Akbar sponsored the rebuilding of a great temple to Shiva but his great grandson Aurangzeb destroyed it again and built a mosque at the site, which now stands beside it. But the traditions of this city go too deep to be uprooted, it has always possessed the will to endure and the temple rose once again.

Benaras Hindu University was founded by Madan Mohan Malviya early this century. He wanted to combine Varanasi's great tradition of Sanskrit scholarship with modern education. Bharat Kala Bhavan located in the University Campus has a good collection of artifacts and medieval miniature paintings. Also within the campus is the new Vishwanath Temple in pristine marble with carved figures and screens that is said to be a replica of the temple destroyed by Aurangzeb. Varanasi's second museum is in the Ramnagar Fort complex across the river.

Varanasi is a city that enjoys the pleasures of this world as much as it thinks of the next. Music and dance have a long history here. Great Hindustani classical musicians like Ustad Bismillah Khan, Pandit Ravi Shankar, Siddeshwari Devi, among others, have come from these lanes. The people have an inimical blend of spiritualism and worldliness in their character and an ability to laugh at life's vissicitudes.

The weavers of Varanasi have been creating exquisite silks and brocades for centuries. Once they were the prized goods being carried on the Silk Route to Europe and to China. Even today Indian brides get married in the silk sarees woven in Varanasi. It is said that the muslin shroud that covered the Buddha after his *Mahaparinirvana* was from Varanasi, and it was woven so fine it would not absorb oil.

A lotus woven in *zari* and silk by the skilled weavers of Varanasi

Birth of the Buddha

On the full moon night of *Vaisakha* (April - May), Mahamaya, the chief queen of King Suddhodana of Kapilavastu, had a beautiful dream. In the dream she saw a six-tusked elephant enter her side as she lay sleeping. The king summoned sixtyfour Brahman astrologers to interpret the dream. They concurred that the queen would give birth to a son who would acquire world renown.

Queen Mahamaya bore the child for ten months and one day expressed a desire to go to her maternal home. The royal entourage camped in the beautiful Lumbini grove, the royal park near Kapilavastu. When the Queen reached out for a branch of a Sal tree the child miraculously came out of her right side.

The attendants sing paeans as the earth is blessed with the Prince Siddhartha's birth

LUMBINI

Lumbini grove, the sacred site of Lord Buddha's birth is today a small village in Nepal, 27 kms from Sonauli on the Indo-Nepal border.

Three hundred years after the *Mahaparinirvana*, Emperor Ashoka visited Lumbini and erected a pillar there. This pillar, though broken, still remains at the site. It is known as the Rummendei Pillar after the earlier name of the place (modern name Rupandhei) in Nepal.

The Chinese traveller, Fa Hien, in the 5th century AD and other travellers and pilgrims were aghast to see that jungles had swallowed the entire place, and nothing existed of the scenic pleasure garden. Excavations beginning in the 19th century have once again drawn attention to this holy place.

Rummendei Pillar
Inscription
(Prakrit language,
Brahmi script)

The beloved of the Gods, the King Piyadassi, when he had been consecrated twenty years, came in person and reverenced the place Buddha Sakyamuni was born. He caused a stone pillar to be erected. As the Lord was born here in the village of Lumbini, he has exempted it from tax, and fixed its contribution [i.e. grain] at one-eight.

The newborn Siddhartha – marble image in the Mayadevi Temple, Lumbini

The heavens filled with light and the *devas* (gods), showered flowers on the young Prince Siddhartha who descended from his mother's womb on a lotus pedestal. The prince took seven strides in all the four directions and announced that this would be his last birth. Queen Mahamaya departed to the heavenly abode soon after giving birth.

An old sage, Asita, prophesied that the prince would become a world renouncer if he ever experienced suffering. To ward off this possibility, Suddhodana ensconced the prince in the royal luxuries of his palace at Kapilavastu, but to no avail. Destiny took its course and Prince Siddhartha renounced his royal heritage and set off on the course to find a solution to end human misery.

The Mayadevi temple and the tank nearby are part of the sacred complex. There are two beautiful panels in the temple, the older one in stone and the other in marble. Both panels show Mayadevi holding the Sal tree and the young prince emerging out of her right side.

Just outside the temple is a tank whose water glistens in the faint sun, the gentle breeze creating endless ripples. Here Queen Mahamaya had her bath before the delivery and it was also here that Prince Siddhartha had his first purificatory bath.

The sacred site of the Buddha's birth is at the southern end of Lumbini grove. Excavations have revealed a series of rooms and a stone slab which is now believed to mark the exact location at which the Buddha was born.

The place where the miraculous birth took place is today a mound that has been cordoned off for further excavations. The whole place has an air of remoteness except when the occasional busload of pilgrims from different corners of the Buddhist universe arrives.

Mayadevi Temple

Lumbini Dharmodaya Samiti Dharmashala, a Theravada Buddhist Vihara, established in 1956, is just outside the complex. Built in the style of modern Nepalese temples, it has intricately carved woodwork in the doorways and windows, and colourful murals depicting events from the life of the Lord in its spacious interiors.

The sacred tank at Lumbini grove

**His Eminence
Chogya Trichen Rinpoche**

Burmese Pagoda

Dharmaswami Maharaja Buddha Vihara, a Tibetan gompa belonging to the Sakyapa Order, is also outside the complex. His Eminence Chogya Trichen Rinpoche and the Raja of Mustang established it. Every morning around sixty monks who reside here conduct the *Tara Puja*. At the end of September, two thousand monks congregate for the ten-day peace *puja* and on 13th December each year for the *Mahakala Puja*, which lasts for 10 days.

A couple of kilometres away, a complex of monasteries is being constructed on a grand scale. Monasteries in the respective national styles of Myanmar (Burma), China, Japan, Korea and Thailand are among those that are being built.

Also in the vicinity are the Lumbini Research Institute, which has an impressive collection of Buddhist literature, and a Museum.

Both are open from Sunday to Saturday, 10 am - 5 pm, 10 am - 4 pm (in winter).

GETTING THERE

Lumbini is in Nepal, 27 kms from the Indian border at Sonauli. To enter Nepal, people from India and Bhutan do not need any visa but foreign nationals do. For details contact the nearest Royal Nepal Embassy in your country or in India.

By Road	Gorakhpur via Sonauli, 123 kms
	Sonauli, 27 kms
	Kushinagar via Gorakhpur, 176 kms
	Kapilavastu (Piprahwa) via Sonauli, 93 kms
Nearest Railhead	Gorakhpur via Sonauli, 123 kms
Nearest Airport	Varanasi, 413 kms
	Bhairawha (Nepal), 13 kms

KAPILAVASTU

The little village of Piprahwa, 93 kms from
Lumbini via Sonauli, is identified as
Kapilavastu, the capital of the Sakyas, where
the Lord spent the first thirty years of his life.
If Lumbini is remote then Kapilavastu seems
to be caught in a time warp.

Excavations were conducted by the
Archaeological Survey of India between 1971
and 1977. In a stupa that was excavated,
referred to as the Eastern Stupa, by
archaeologists, an inscription was found
dating back to the Kushan period. Its text read
Om devaputra vihare Kapilavastu bhikku sanghasa
(This is the Devaputra Vihara of the
Kapilavastu *bhikshu sangha*).

One and a half kilometres from the site there
are two excavated mounds. The larger one is a
thick walled structure, which according to
local belief, was Suddhodana's palace.

There is a small Sri Lankan monastery and
temple, Mahinda Mahavihara, in the vicinity
of the ruins.

Amidst the ruins of Kapilavastu

The image of Lord Buddha in the Bhumisparsha Mudra or the earth touching pose, housed in the diamond throne chamber of the Mahabodhi Temple – the holiest of all Buddhist shrines

I had once gone on a visit to Bodh Gaya, and it had thrilled me to think that he who had hallowed the earth by the touch of his feet had once come to that very place in the flesh. Why, I had thought with a pang, had I not been born in this day, that I might have received his holy influence directly with all my mind and all my body.

Rabindranath Tagore 1935

BODH GAYA

Bodh Gaya, is located in Bihar, 115 kms from Patna. The land is rich and fertile, dotted with green fields, watered by the river Phalgu (ancient Nairanjana). A range of low forested hills silhouette the small hamlets flanking the glistening, sandy banks of the river.

Here more than 2500 years ago came Siddhartha, a young ascetic, having renounced royal heritage. He was looking for a quiet retreat where he could meditate upon the causes for human suffering. He had faced many trials and tribulations in his search for Truth. As he gazed across the river Phalgu upon the serene landscape of Uruvela village (modern Bodh Gaya) he knew his quest had ended. The kind daughter of the village chief of Senani, Sujata, brought a bowl of *kheer* (sweet thickened milk) for the starved ascetic. It is said that the gods had infused the *kheer* with ambrosia.

Quiet flows the Nairanjana river

Siddhartha spread *kusha* grass beneath the Bodhi or Bo tree (Pipal tree; botanical name, *ficus religiosia*) and sat cross-legged facing the east with a vow to get up only if he attained supreme knowledge. For 49 days Mara, the temptor, assaulted him with his weapons of flood, fire, thunder and lightening. Then Mara's three beautiful daughters tried to allure him, but in vain. He entered deeper states of contemplation. His quest finally ended at dawn on *Vaisakha Poornima*, the full moon day in April-May. He had attained *Samma Sambodhi*, the Enlightenment that he had been seeking for so long. He was no more a seeker or Bodhisattva. He had become the Buddha.

> *Through many a birth in Samsara wandered I,*
> *Seeking but not finding, the builder of this house.*
> *Sorrowful is repeated birth.*
> *O house-builder! You are seen.*
> *You shall build no house again.*
> *All your rafters are broken, your ridgepole is shattered.*
> *To nirvana goes my mind. Achieved is the end of craving.*

Dhammapada 153, 154

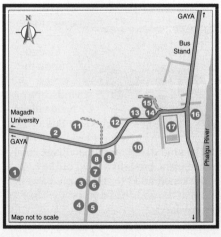

1 Root Institute for Culture & Wisdom
2 Vietnamese Monastery
3 Daijokyo Japanese Monastery
4 Great Buddha Statue
5 Sakya Tibetan Monastery
6 Indosan Nipponji Temple
7 Bhutanese Monastery
8 Thai Temple
9 Nepali Temple
10 Archaeological Museum

To prostrate simply is also to meditate

As the place of the Buddha's Enlightenment, Bodh Gaya is the spiritual home of Buddhists. It attracts tens of thousands of believers from all over the world. Shaven heads, billowing ochre and maroon robes, monks and nuns, a string of beads in hand, rub shoulders with sari and jeans clad locals and tourists from across the globe. An all-pervading calm envelops the town, casting a peaceful spell on the visitor.

A novice being tonsured, severing one more link with the material world

77

MAHABODHI MAHAVIHARA

Set among verdant lawns, the magnificent 52 metre high sandstone Mahabodhi Temple soars towards the blue skies. The Bodhi tree on the left is surrounded by small beautifully carved votive stupas and chaityas and numerous images of the Buddha. Prayer flags flutter in the sky, spreading the message of the Master. At daybreak not a whisper, not a sound is heard, except for the gentle rustle of the Bodhi leaves and an occassional murmur of *mantras*.

Above:
Colourful prayer flags whisper the Master's message to the gentle wind

Left:
Tall stands the Mahabodhi Temple beckoning believers from across the continents

Right:
Votive stupas dot the sunken courtyard at the Mahabodhi Temple

79

Buddhapada in the Mahabodhi Temple depicts the chakras (wheels) on the soles of the Lord's feet – one of the thirtytwo auspicious signs of a great person

As the day dawns, devotees and laymen pour in. A flight of steps leads to the inner courtyard through a beautifully carved granite *torana* (gateway). A large circular stone with the Buddha's footprints or *Buddhapada* is kept in a small shrine on the left. The Mahabodhi Temple stands in the centre, crowned by a pointed spire flanked by four corner turrets. The main shrine chamber rests on a plinth 8 metre high. The sanctum houses a gilded statue of the Buddha in the *bhumisparsha mudra* with one finger touching the earth, calling it to witness his awakening. The air is filled with the heady fragrance of incense and flowers.

Special offerings to the Bodhi tree

A chamber at the top houses a figure of Mayadevi, the Buddha's mother. Outside in the sunken courtyard, people pray, meditate and prostrate before the Bodhi tree and the Mahabodhi Temple, making a wish or in thanksgiving.

At night in the golden light of butter lamps and candles, the shimmering leaves of the Bodhi tree and the glittering stones of the temple radiate the Master's universal message of love and compassion, charity and selflessness.

On this site once stood a temple built by the Mauryan emperor, Ashoka, around the 3rd century BC. Excavations around the present temple have revealed foundations of a small Vihara called the Prachin Vajrasan Gandhakuti Vihara. The temple was rebuilt in 7th century AD by the Pala kings of Bengal. Hiuen Tsang, the Chinese scholar pilgrim, refers to having seen it.

The temple was destroyed by Muslim invaders in the 12th century. The Burmese kings restored it in the 14th century. However, the temple complex was severely flooded and remained buried under silt till 1811. Alexander Cunningham, Director General of the Archaeological Survey of India, visited the site in 1861 and recommended excavations.

In 1891 a Sri Lankan Buddhist, Anagarika Dharmapala, founded the Mahabodhi Society of India whose avowed goal was to wrest the Bodh Gaya temple from Hindu priests and reclaim it for the Buddhists. On 23rd May, 1953, the temple was finally handed over to Dr S Radhakrishnan, the then Vice President of India.

Seven spots within the precincts of the Mahabodhi Temple are specially sacred because it was at these spots that the Buddha spent a week each, meditating, after his Enlightenment. Visitors tread these grounds reverentially and carefully because of their association with the Great Master.

The spire of the Mahabodhi Temple stands resplendent against an azure blue sky and flaming gulmohar flowers

The Buddha spent the first week under the Bodhi tree. It is believed that the original tree sprang up the day the Buddha was born. The tree was destroyed and replanted at least five times. The present tree grew from a sapling brought from the tree in Anuradhapura in Sri Lanka which was planted there by Emperor Ashoka's son Mahendra in the 3rd century BC. Poet-philosopher Ashwaghosha who wrote the *Buddhacharita* called it the navel of the earth. The *vajrasana* or diamond throne, a red sandstone slab, is kept at the spot where the Buddha sat in meditation under the Bodhi tree.

The Vajrasana is the place where the Buddhas attain the holy path. It is also called Bodhi manda. When the great earth is shaken, this place alone is unmoved. Therefore when Tathagata was about to reach the condition of Enlightenment, and he went successively to the four angles of this enclosure, the earth shook and quaked; but afterwards coming to this spot all was still and at rest.

Hiuen Tsang 7th century AD

Carved railings of granite and sandstone enclose the Mahabodhi Temple and the Bodhi tree. The original railings belonging to the Sunga period, 184-72 BC, have been removed to the Bodh Gaya Museum, the Indian Museum, Calcutta and the Victoria and Albert Museum, London.

Ratnachankrama

The Master spent the second week at the Animeshlochana Chaitya, from where he gazed at the Bodhi tree without blinking (*animesha*).

The Ratnachankrama or jewel walk is where the Lord spent the third week walking between the Bodhi tree and the Animeshlochana Chaitya. Where the Master's feet rested, lotus flowers sprang up.

Not by matted hair, nor by family, nor by birth does one become a Brahman. But in whom there exists both Truth and Righteousness, pure is he, a Brahman is he.

   Dhammapada 393

The Buddha spent the fourth week in the Ratnaghar Chaitya where he reflected on the higher modes of exposition, *Abhidharma Nyaya*. Blue, yellow, red, white and orange rays emanated from the Master's body as he meditated. The Buddhist flag therefore uses these colours. The fifth week was spent in the east, near the entrance. Under a Banyan tree in response to a Brahman's query, he expounded that good *karma* and not birth makes a *Brahman*. The Lord spent the sixth week at the Muchhalinda pond on the southern side of the temple.

Muchhalinda pond – here the serpent king, Muchhalinda, protected the Buddha from a severe storm

The seventh and the last week was spent in the southeast where under the Rajyatna tree the Buddha preached his doctrines.

The Ratnaghar Chaitya – where the Buddha meditated for higher wisdom

(Mahabodhi Temple is open 5 am-9 pm. Video camera fee Rs 100 per day. Still camera fee Rs 5 per entry. Film shooting fee Rs 500 per day).

An ornate image of Maitreya – the future Buddha

MONASTERIES

Bodh Gaya is quite an international town as monasteries, guest houses, meditation centres and Buddhist temples of different countries abound. These are traditionally built and decorated with colourful images and Buddhist symbols.

Across the road from the Mahabodhi Temple is the Mahabodhi Society of India and the old Tibetan monastery. The first floor of the monastery houses a figure of the Maitreya Buddha (future Buddha) and is decorated with Tibetan scriptures, *tangkha*s and other religious objects. A room downstairs has a huge Wheel of Law weighing over 20 tonnes.

There are two Japanese temples, old and new, and here too are graceful and elegant gilded images of the Buddha in the earth touching pose.

Set in the midst of a garden, the beautiful Thai temple was built in the pagoda style in 1956. Traditionally decorated, it houses an opulent, gilded figure of the Buddha in the earth touching pose.

The Royal Bhutanese and the New Tibetan Gompas are examples of the artistic skill of the Northern School. Traditional religious symbols, motifs, and designs have been painted in bright, contrasting colours. Inside are life size statues of the Buddha, outlined in gold.

(Timings: Monasteries are open from 7 am - 12 pm; 2 pm - 5 pm)

Nineteen and half metre high statue of the Buddha in *dhyani mudra* or Meditating posture

FESTIVALS

Bodh Gaya, the holiest of all Buddhist pilgrimages, draws devotees all the year round. Pilgrims attend the Buddha Jayanti celebrations on the full moon night in the month of *Vaisakha* in April-May when the temperature touches 45°C. The entire town celebrates the event with prayer meets, religious discourses, group meditation, processions and symposia. The Mahabodhi Temple wears a festive look, specially decorated with colourful flags and flowers.

The other important occasions are the birth anniversary of Anagarika Dharmapala, 17th September, the birth and death anniversaries of Babasaheb Ambedkar, 14th April and 6th December, and Hiroshima Day on 6th August.

The Vajrasana or the Diamond Throne under the Bodhi tree where the Lord sat for fortynine days until he attained Nirvana

The Kalachakra ceremony is held for about ten days each year and presided over by His Holiness the XIVth Dalai Lama, the spiritual and temporal head of Tibetan Buddhists. It is believed that if one attends this ceremony at least once in a lifetime one will attain salvation. Since 1994 the American branch of the Tibetan Nyingmapa sect holds a Peace Ceremony with a view to promoting peace and goodwill among mankind.

Impressions of the *Buddhapada* on cloth – a sacred souvenir

BODH GAYA MUSEUM

Bodh Gaya Museum of the Archaeological Survey of India is located near the Mahabodhi temple. It houses antiquities excavated in and around Bodh Gaya.

(Open 9 am to 4.30 pm. Closed: Fridays. Entry: Rs 2)

Two elaborately carved votive stupas.
Top: From Bodh Gaya Museum, Pala period, eastern India.
Right: In the sacred complex of Mahabodhi Temple – a part of the living tradition.

GETTING THERE

By Road	Gaya, 16 kms
	Dobhi, 22 kms on the Delhi-Calcutta Grand Trunk Road (NH 2)
	Patna, 115 kms via Jehanabad, and 181 kms via Rajgir
	Rajgir, 70 kms
Nearest Railhead	Gaya, 16 kms on the Calcutta-Delhi main line
Nearest Airport	Patna 112 kms

EXCURSIONS

Vishnupad Mandir in Gaya is 15 kms away. Situated on the banks of river Phalgu, the temple was built by Rani Ahalya Bai Holkar of Indore in 1787 and houses the footprints of Lord Vishnu engraved on solid rock. Hindu pilgrims come here all the year round to perform the last rites of their dead ancestors and offer funeral cakes or *pindas,* which ensures their salvation.

Brahmayoni Hill or Gayasirsa is 1 km away to the southwest of Gaya. Here in the Pragbodhi caves Prince Siddhartha practiced severe austerities. He later returned to preach the Fire Sermon which extols celibacy and a lust free life.

Barabar is 42 kms from Gaya and 12 kms east of Bela railway station on the Patna-Gaya highway. It is famous for its seven rock-cut caves, in addition to the three in the nearby Nagarjuna hills belonging to the Mauryan period and dedicated to the Ajivika sect. These ancient caves are hewn out of single granite rocks. Some chambers have exquisitely polished interiors. Barabar is remarkable for its sheer panoramic grandeur, rugged landscape and serene charm.

Lomas Rishi cave in Barabar, with its ornamental arched entrance

[In Sarnath] is a lake about 150 paces round… The water is deep
and its taste sweet; it is pure and resplendent in appearance…
When men of a bad character bathe here, crocodiles come forth and
kill many of them; but in case of the reverential who wash here,
they need fear nothing.

Hiuen Tsang 7th century AD

SARNATH

The presence of the Great Teacher permeates the quiet ruins of Sarnath. The still air carries the fragrance of incense and flowers and the chants of the monks. Deer wander among the ruins and spiders weave huge spreading webs in the grass that shimmers at dawn, spangled with dew.

Sarnath is only 10 kms from Varanasi, the holy city of the Hindus. After the frenetic volatility of Varanasi, also called Benaras and Kashi, Sarnath welcomes you with a serene smile.

After Sakyamuni gained Enlightenment under the Bodhi tree on the banks of the Nairanjana river, he walked for over 250 kms from Bodh Gaya, crossed the Ganga by ferry to reach the *ghats* of Kashi. He was searching for the five companions who had abandoned him at Rajgir. The five ascetics deserted him when Gautama forsook the path of self-mortification because they felt that spiritual salvation was not possible through any other means.

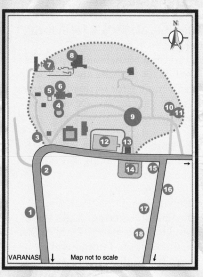

1	Japanese Temple
2	Archaeological Museum
3	Ticket Office
4	Dharmarajika Stupa
5	Ashoka's Column
6	Main Shrine
7	Monastery Ruins
8	Monastery Ruins
9	Dhamekh Stupa
10	Mulgandhakuti Vihara
11	Bodhi Tree
12	Jain Digambar Temple
13	Maitreya Buddha Temple
14	Mahabodhi Society of India
15	Auto Rickshaw Stand
16	Chinese Temple
17	UP Tourist Bungalow/ Restaurant
18	Post Office

The Buddha found the five ascetics at a deer park in the outskirts of the city. The park was called Rishipattana or Issipattana after the *rishis* or sages who came to meditate under its shady trees. Its other name was Mrigadaya or deer sanctuary, because a king of Varanasi had gifted the land as a safe haven for deer. The modern name of Sarnath is derived from the name of the Bodhisattva, Saranganatha.

The Wheel of Dharma – set in motion at Sarnath

The Blessed One met his old companions who were the first to hear him unfold his path to Enlightenment, the Four Noble Truths, the Eightfold Path and the Middle Way. This first sermon is called *Dharmachakrapravartana*, or Turning of the Wheel of Law.

The end of suffering is Enlightenment, *Nirvana*.
What is the truth of Suffering, (*dukkha*)?
Birth is suffering, decay, sickness and death are suffering ...
In short, the human personality, prone as it is to attachment, brings suffering.

What is the truth of the Cause of Suffering?
It is craving.
Craving leads to rebirth, bound up as this is with the search for pleasure and restless greed. It is in craving for sensuality, craving for new life, craving for non-existence and annihilation.

What is the truth of the End of Suffering?
It is the elimination of craving: freedom and detachment from it.

What is the Noble Eightfold Path which leads to the End of Suffering? Right View, Right Thought, Right Speech, Right Action, Right Livelihood, Right Effort, Right Mindfulness, and Right Concentration.

At Sarnath the Buddha founded the *Sangha* with his five old companions as his first disciples. It was also here that Yasa, the son of a rich merchant of Kashi, renounced his life of worldly pleasures to become Sakyamuni's disciple. Kondanna, leader of the first converts, described the moment of his realisation:
Lo! he hath passed with vigour out and on;
Sloughed off hath he the dyings and the births,
Wholly accomplishing the life sublime.

The Lord delivering the first sermon at Sarnath

Thereafter for 45 years the Lord walked the dusty plains of northern India, touching the lives of millions with his teachings. However he did not forget Sarnath. He came back to the Deer Park to meditate during the months of the next monsoon and for many other such retreats.

Sarnath gained eminence during the reign of Emperor Ashoka. The Ashoka Pillar and its famous lion capital were discovered in 1904. Later Saka and Kushan monarchs also patronised Buddhist monks and promoted Buddhist art in Sarnath. However, in the 12th century both Varanasi and Sarnath faced the first onslaught of Muslim invasion. After Qutbuddin Aibak's attack in 1194, the thriving monastery in Sarnath lay in ruins, and the few monks who survived, fled.

Sarnath never rose again. The faith survived in other countries but Sarnath no longer echoed to the chants of the monks.

Beautiful Buddha images in the niches of the votive stupas

Seven hundred years later, in 1834, a British archaeological team led by Alexander Cunningham rediscovered Sarnath, opening a window to a forgotten period of India's ancient history.

Today the ruined stupas, broken walls of monastery cells and statues within the niches of the walls, lie within stretches of emerald lawns.

DHAMEKH STUPA

The most impressive sight in Sarnath is the looming pile of the Dhamekh Stupa, possibly built around 500AD. It was built at the site of many earlier constructions as excavations reveal brickwork from much earlier periods. Dhamekh Stupa is a solid cylindrical tower, 33 metres in height. The borders have delicately carved geometrical and floral patterns and the figures of humans and birds.

The base of the Stupa is made of stone with the upper areas of brickwork which probably once had a carved stone fencing.

The present name Dhamekh shows some connection with Buddha's *Dharma*. This might indeed have been the stupa built by Ashoka to mark the spot where the Buddha preached the *Dharmachakrapravartana* for the first time to the five ascetics.

The magnificent Dhamekh Stupa, a towering presence in the Deer Park

Inset: Intricate floral and geometrical patterns on the Dhamekh Stupa

DHARMARAJIKA STUPA

Dharmarajika Stupa marks the site where the Buddha gave his first sermon. It was broken down in the 18th century by an officer of the Maharaja of Benaras who was looking for building material for constructing a bazaar. A marble casket was found beneath the stupa during excavations by Alexander Cunningham in the late 19th century.

Just behind the Dharmarajika Stupa are the remains of the massive Ashoka Pillar, one of the many that Emperor Ashoka set up at Buddhist sites. It is placed at the spot where the Buddha gave his first sermon and established the *Sangha*. The monolithic Ashoka Pillar was once crowned with the magnificent Lion Capital, which is now kept in the Sarnath Museum. The four roaring lions face the four cardinal directions symbolising the spread of the Buddha's teachings.

The lions originally supported the *dharmachakra* or the wheel of law but only a few fragments of it have been found. In the lower portion of the column are carved a lotus, four smaller wheels, and a lion, bull, horse and an elephant. The original pillar was over 15 metres tall but only a stump remains standing near the Dhamekh Stupa. The carved inscription is a warning by Emperor Ashoka to the monks and nuns against creating schisms within the Order.

MULGANDHAKUTI VIHARA

Mulgandhakuti marks the site where the Buddha meditated during his monsoon retreats at Sarnath. Excavations have unearthed a statue of a Bodhisattva from the 1st century AD, and a tablet on which the name of the shrine was carved. In 1922, Anagarika Dharmapala laid the foundation of a temple named Mulgandhakuti Vihara at the site. It enshrines relics of the Buddha which were discovered at Taxila. The interior has frescoes painted by a Japanese artist in 1932-35.

Mulgandhakuti Vihara – a favourite retreat of the Buddha during the *vassavasa*

Outside is the Bodhi tree and its spreading branches symbolise the return of Buddhism to India.

CHAUKHANDI

The first landmark that visitors see on their way to Sarnath from Varanasi is a high mound with the remains of a brick stupa built in the Gupta period. Today the site is called Chaukhandi. It marks the spot where the Buddha first met his five companions on arriving in Sarnath. A Mughal style octagonal tower was added by Govardhan, son of Raja Todar Mal, in 1588, to celebrate a visit by the Mughal Emperor Akbar to the city.

FESTIVALS

Buddha *Poornima*, the full moon night in April - May, when the birth of the Buddha is celebrated, is the biggest festival at Sarnath. There are prayers, processions and pageantry, with pilgrims coming from all over the world. A big fair also springs up on the occasion. During the first full moon in November an assembly of monks and scholars celebrate the anniversary of the foundation of the Mulgandhakuti Vihara.

GETTING THERE

By Road	Varanasi, 10 kms
	Bodh Gaya via Mohania, 240 kms
Nearest Railhead	Varanasi, 10 kms, and Mughal Sarai Junction, 16 kms. Both are well connected with Patna, Delhi, Bombay, Calcutta and Madras
Nearest Airport	Varanasi Airport at Babatpur, 22 kms from Varanasi

SARNATH MUSEUM

The Sarnath Museum is a treasure trove of Buddhist sculptures, inscriptions and pottery. Some of the finest images of the Buddha and panels depicting important episodes from the life of Sakyamuni can be seen here. The largest collection is from the Gupta period, carved in the fine-grained Chunar sandstone.

In Sarnath Museum one can see the magnificent Lion Capital, which once crowned the Ashoka Pillar at Sarnath and which today is the official symbol of the Indian State.

A fine example of the Mathura School of Art from the Kushan period (1st century AD) is the standing image of the Buddha in red sandstone, with exquisitely carved details. There is also a beautiful image of a serene Buddha, the smiling lips and half shut eyelids creating an aura of compassion and meditative calm. Six figures kneel at his feet and the decorated halo behind his head has two flying celestial figures among the floral patterns.

The lion capital – India's national emblem, a tribute to the Buddha's teachings

The library of the Mahabodhi Society possesses an excellent collection of Buddhist literature and rare manuscripts. There is also a fascinating sculpture shed, which displays finds from past excavations.

All Buddhist nations have their monasteries and temples in Sarnath, built in the indigenous architectural styles of the respective countries.

EXCURSIONS

Kaushambi was the capital of the famous Vatsa Mahajanapada, during the time of the Lord. The Buddha is said to have visited this place in the sixth and ninth years after the Enlightenment and delivered several sermons. He stayed in the Ghositarama Vihara, which has been excavated recently. Hiuen Tsang visited this place after visiting Prayag (Allahabad) 54 kms away, which continues to be the nearest railhead. Allahabad is well connected by train to Varanasi, which also has the closest airport to Kaushambi.

Rajagriha with its beautiful palaces is distinguished by the five hills, well guarded and adorned with mountains, supported and hallowed by auspicious sacred places.

Aswaghosha *Buddhacharita* 1st century AD

1	Jivakamravana
2	Ropeway Stand
3	Griddhakuta Hill
4	Vishwa Shanti Stupa
5	Bimbisar's Jail
6	Satdhara Hot Spring
7	Pippala Cave
8	Saptaparni Cave
9	Venuvana Vihara
10	Karanda Tank
11	Tathagata Hotel
12	Virayatan
13	Centaur Hokke Hotel
14	Ajatshatru Stupa

RAJGIR

The meandering river Banganga and five hills ensconce picturesque Rajgir, ancient Rajagriha (literally, the abode of kings). During the lifetime of the Buddha this was the capital of the powerful Magadhan kingdom, ruled by the virtuous King Bimbisara. The hills and caves surrounding Rajagriha were home to spiritual teachers, ranging from the materialism of the early Charavaka school to the metaphysics of Upanishadic philosophers. Like many others in search of Truth, Prince Siddhartha, after he renounced his royal heritage came to this city to seek the path of salvation.

Siddhartha overwhelmed the citizens of Rajagriha with his serenity and grace. Even the king went to meet the ascetic and was amazed to learn that he was a *kshatriya* of royal descent. Bimbisara offered half his kingdom to Siddhartha but all he received was an assurance that when Siddhartha achieved his goal he would return to Rajagriha.

Gilded image of the Buddha in a niche of the Vishwa Shanti Stupa

Deign [to bestow upon] us a portion of it,
when you obtain the supreme sanctity!
And bowing his head to [the Bodhisattva's] feet,
[Bimbisara] made a circumambulation, and went back.

Lalitavistara 14th century AD

Hundred kilometres southeast of Patna, Rajgir is connected by an excellent road to Patna as well as to Bodh Gaya, which is 70 kms away. The ancient university, Nalanda, is just 11 kms from here. The town's many attractions draw both pilgrims and tourists. It is advisable to hire your own vehicle. The town also boasts the largest number of horse drawn carriages or *tongas* anywhere in India.

The Cyclopean walls made of dry unhewn stone blocks were once pierced by 32 large and 64 smaller gates

Entering Rajgir from Bodh Gaya one glimpses the remains of the Cyclopean walls which extend from the east to the west, from one hill to another. Once 40 kms long, these walls encircled the city built by Bimbisara.

Off the main road, towards the south are the venerated Griddhakuta Hill, or Vulture Peak, and Ratnagiri. The metalled road follows the path originally laid by Bimbisara as a footway through the jungle.

Remains of brick shrines and monasteries on Griddhakuta peak

A ropeway takes pilgrims to Ratnagiri, crowned by the brilliant white Vishwa Shanti Stupa.

The Vishwa Shanti Stupa is a marble structure with niches bearing golden images of the Buddha, built by the Nipponzan Myohoji sect of Japan. Opposite the Stupa stands the Saddharma Buddha Vihara.

A fifteen minute walk from Vishwa Shanti Stupa leads to Griddhakuta, sanctified by the Master's presence. The strange rock protrusion resembling a vulture's beak probably gave the hill its name. In the rock cut caves here the Buddha spent many rainy seasons, meditating and preaching.

The 38 metre high Vishwa Shanti Stupa is the 22nd in the chain of shrines built to propagate world peace.

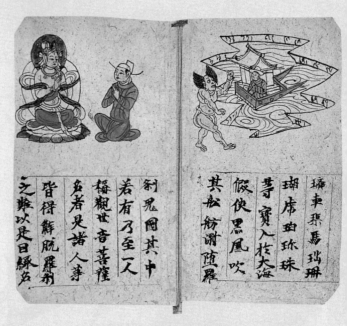

It was at Griddhakuta that the Enlightened One delivered the Lotus Sutra, which promises salvation for all beings. At the heart of this *sutra* is the compassion of the Buddha whose concern is with earthly suffering – each of us may attain Enlightenment, whoever may have folded their hands or uttered *namo* to the Buddha.

An early 10th century illustrated Chinese manuscript of the Lotus Sutra, from the Dunhuang Caves in China

The Buddha also delivered the Prajnaparamita or Perfection of Wisdom Sutra at Griddhakuta.

Therefore, the mantra of the perfection of wisdom is a mantra of great knowledge;
It is an unsurpassable mantra; it is a mantra that totally pacifies all sufferings.
It will not deceive you, therefore know it to be true!
I proclaim the mantra of the perfection of wisdom:

Tayatha gate gate paragate parasamgate bodhi svaha.

Lord Buddha subdues the elephant. 12th century illuminated palm leaf manuscript from eastern India.

The easy climb down from Griddhakuta Hill crosses the site of Mardakukshi Vihara. It was here that Bimbisara's queen tried to get rid of her unborn child when it was prophesied that her son would one day kill his father. The Enlightened One was first brought here when he was wounded by a rock hurled by his envious cousin Devadatta.

Along the road to the new town built by Ajatashatru are the ruins of Jivakamravana Vihara, the mango grove presented to the Buddha by Jivaka, the royal physician, who cared for the Lord after he was injured by Devadatta. Stone foundations of large elliptical halls and subsidiary rooms suggest the existence of a large monastery.

Across the road are the remains of the jail where Bimbisara was imprisoned and killed by his son, Ajatashatru. From here the unfortunate king could see the Master as he meditated on Griddhakuta. Ajatashatru, along with Devadatta, had conspired to take the life of the Lord by letting loose a mad elephant. But the Lord tamed the wild elephant which stood still, overcome by the Lord's serene visage. After killing his father, Ajatashatru was filled with remorse and later embraced the faith.

Ruins of the Jivakamravana Vihara

Karanda Tank

A couple of kilometres away is Venuvana Vihara or the Monastery of the Bamboo Grove. This was Bimbisara's first offering to Lord Buddha. Close by is the Karanda Tank where the Buddha bathed.

Ajatashatru Stupa

On the road leading to Nalanda can be seen the ruins of Ajatashatru Fort. Towards the west, excavations have revealed the ruins of Ajatashatru Stupa, buil ver his share of the relics of the Buddha.

Rajagriha sank into oblivion when Ajatashatru's son, Udayin, shifted the capital to Pataliputra (modern Patna).

Rajgir is also famous for its seven hot sulphur springs, Satadhara. Situated at the foot of Vaibhava Hill it is a ten minute walk from Venuvana. The hot springs are a part of the Lakshminarayan Temple complex.

On the hills above are the Pippala caves, hewn into the stone platform, popularly known as Jarasandh ki Baithak after the mythical Hindu king Jarasandh. A rocky path from Pippala caves leads to the seven caves of Saptaparni, where the First Buddhist Council was held to codify the teachings of the Great Master.

Sonebhandar Caves

Rajgir is also sacred to the followers of the Jain religion. Vardhaman Mahavira, the 24th Tirthankara, spent 14 rainy seasons here and many of the hilltops are crowned with Jain temples.

A short drive from Venuvana Vihara leads to Virayatna, a Jain *ashram*, with a residential area and a museum.

The cylindrical Jain shrine of the Maniyar Math is decorated with stucco figures. The Sonebhandar caves, a short distance from Maniyar Math were built by the Jain saint Vairadeva.

GETTING THERE	
By Road	Patna, 100 kms Bodh Gaya, 70 kms Nalanda, 11 kms
Nearest Railhead	Bhakhtiyarpur, 54 kms, on the Delhi-Howrah main line
Nearest Airport	Patna, 100 kms

Monks circumambulating the Sariputra Stupa

Should one recite a hundred verses with useless words, better is one single beneficial word of the Dharma, by hearing which one is pacified.

Though he should conquer a thousand men in the battlefield, yet he, indeed is the noblest victor who would conquer himself.

Dhammapada 102,103

NALANDA

Silence reigns supreme, gradually the early morning sun lifts the mantle of darkness. In its golden light, the scores of ruined red brick buildings set amongst lush green lawns appear almost ethereal. There is no sign of life today except for a few curious visitors. But once the place throbbed with life, its corridors reverberated with eager voices engrossed in the pursuit of knowledge. This is Nalanda, the most renowned university in ancient India. It derived its name from *Na-alam-da*, meaning Insatiable in Giving, one of the names by which the Lord Buddha was known. Today it is identified with modern Baragaon village and is 90 kms southeast of Patna and only 11 kms from Rajgir. It is 80 kms from Bodh Gaya and is easily accessible by well-maintained highways.

The monastic university, Nalanda Mahavihara, was a magnificent architectural structure. An inscription of King Yashovarman of 7th century AD describes Nalanda as "rows of monasteries with their series of turrets licking the clouds."

The mammoth brickfaced Sariputra Stupa is surrounded by numerous smaller votive stupas

The Buddha came to Nalanda often and stayed at Setthi Pavarika's mango grove. Two of Sakyamuni's chief disciples, Sariputra and Maudgalyayana, came from the vicinity of Nalanda. Sariputra, who was considered the foremost in wisdom and had a very important place in the *Sangha*, attained *Nirvana* here. Emperor Ashoka came to Nalanda to worship at the chaitya of Sariputra and built another temple over the existing shrine. Fa Hien mentions having seen this stupa.

It was at this sanctified site that the Mahavihara was first established in the reign of Emperor Kumargupta in the 5th century AD, a tradition carried forward by his successors in the Gupta dynasty. During the reign of Devapala in the beginning of the 9th century, Nalanda reached its zenith of fame and glory. Emissaries from around the world came with rich presents and generous donations to Nalanda, as they did to other contemporary Buddhist universities like Odantapuri, a stone's throw away from Nalanda, and Vikramshila, in Bhagalpur district of Bihar.

Scholars converged on this blessed place, once traversed by the Buddha, thirsting for *Dharma*. Hiuen Tsang and later his disciple Hwui Li, who studied at this great institution in the 6th and 7th centuries, have left behind detailed descriptions. Admission was extremely coveted and only two out of ten eminent scholars were admitted.

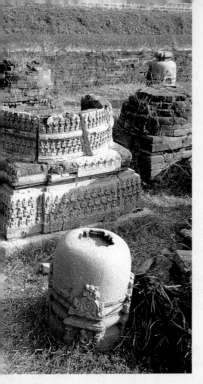

The art of debate (*vada*) and public speaking, and secular subjects like mathematics and medicine were taught here. Doctrinal points were continually debated and debating was a necessary part of monastic education. Among the renowned Indian scholars trained at Nalanda were Nagarjuna, Aryadeva and Asanga. Santarakshita, and thereafter Padmasambhava, went to Tibet from Nalanda to spread the teachings of Sakyamuni.

The Nalanda Mahavihara complex is strewn with many intricately carved votive stupas

A massive fire, schisms between the different Buddhist sects and the resurgence of devotional Hinduism pushed Nalanda to the brink of destruction. Its final nemesis came with the Muslim invader Bakhtiyar Khalji who brutally wiped it off the map. A few valuable manuscripts were rescued from Nalanda's famed libraries by some of the monks who were able to flee from the onslaught.

By far the most beautiful of all excavated monuments is Temple Site 2 with a moulded plinth and sculpted panels revealing 211 figures of gods and goddesses besides dancers, musicians, warriors, animals and birds.

Nalanda is today a World Heritage Site. Excavations in the 1860s by Alexander

Cunningham led to the dicovery of the official seal with the inscription *Sri Nalanda Mahavihara Arya Bhikshu Sanghasya* (Venerable Community of Monks in the Great Vihara of Sri Nalanda).

Nalanda is spread out over an area of 14 hectares and has the ruins of 11 monasteries and 5 temples. Stone paved pathways criss-cross the entire site. Sariputra's Stupa is the most imposing structure standing in the south, a few minutes walk from the main gate. This large stupa was built over the mortal remains of Sariputra. Its corner towers display niches holding well modelled stucco figures of the Buddha and Bodhisattvas. A flight of steps leads to the shrine chamber which once housed a colossal image of Lord Buddha.

A niche in t Sariputra Stupa with Buddha in *bhumispars mudra*

The monastic remains show a number of small cells with wide verandahs in the front, set around open quadrangular courts.

A panoramic view of the monastery at Nalanda

Each complex had a main shrine housing a large figure of the Buddha. Huge ovens were also excavated suggesting that there was a common kitchen for students.

The Archaeological Survey of India maintains the Nalanda Museum across the road which houses some exquisite bronzes of the 9th and 10th centuries, Pala dynasty, and other remains excavated at the site.

Nalanda Mahavihara site is open from 6 am to 5.30 pm daily and the Museum from 10 am to 5 pm. Entry fee is Rs 2 for the Museum and Rs 5 for the site. Entry to the site is free on Fridays but the Museum remains closed on Friday. Video photography charges are Rs 25.

The beautiful Thai Temple and the Nava Nalanda Mahavihara, a centre for research in Pali and Buddhist studies, are 2 kms from the main site.

The new memorial to commemorate the visit of Hiuen Tsang

GETTING THERE	
By Road	Patna, 90 kms
	Rajgir, 11 kms
	Bodh Gaya, 80 kms
Nearest Railhead	Bhakhtiyarpur, 38 kms, on Delhi-Howrah main line
Nearest Airport	Patna, 93 kms

And the rulers and citizens of many countries vied with one another in making offerings at Jetavana Vihara, hanging silk pennants and canopies, scattering flowers and lighting lamps, which burnt day and night without ever being extinguished.

Fa Hien
5th century AD

SRAVASTI

Sravasti (ancient Savatthi), the capital of Kosala Mahajanapada, was the biggest town in the Gangetic plains during the Buddha's lifetime. Sravasti was host to the Master for 25 years during the annual *vassavasa* (rain retreat) when the *Sangha* congregated at one place.

Situated in Gonda district in eastern Uttar Pradesh, Sravasti is also called Sahet-Mahet. The most convenient way to reach Sravasti is via Lucknow, the capital of Uttar Pradesh, which is well connected by air and rail to all parts of India.

A sandstone panel from Bharhut in central India, showing the purchase of the Jetavana Vihara in Sravasti

During the time of Sakyamuni, Sudatta, a rich and pious merchant, lived in Sravasti. While on a visit to Rajgir, he heard the Buddha's sermon and decided to become the Lord's disciple. But he was caught in a dilemma and asked the Lord whether he could become a follower without forsaking worldly life. To his query, the Master replied that it was enough that he followed his vocation in a righteous manner.

Not by a shaven head does an undisciplined man
Who utters lies, become an ascetic.
How will one be an ascetic who is full of desire and greed?
He who wholly subdues evil - both small and great - is called an
ascetic, because he has overcome all evil.

Dhammapada 264, 265

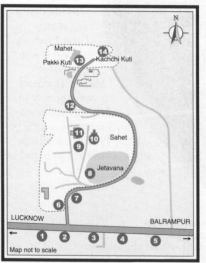

1 UP Tourist Bungalow
2 Thai Temple/Monastery
3 Sri Lankan Guest House
4 Jain Temple
5 Japanese Bell Temple
6 Ticket Office
7 Sri Lankan Temple
8 Anandabodhi Tree
9 Anandakuti
10 Ancient Wall
11 Gandhakuti
12 Chinese Temple
13 Pakki Kuti
     (Angulimala's Stupa)
14 Kachchi Kuti
     (Sudatta's Stupa)

Sudatta invited the Lord to Sravasti and began to look for a suitable place to build a vihara. A beautiful park at the southern edge of Sravasti attracted his attention. The park belonged to Jeta, son of the king of Sravasti, Prasenjit. Jeta demanded that Sudatta cover the entire park with gold coins. Sudatta painstakingly paved every inch of the land with gold. Then Jeta said that since the trees were left uncovered they belonged to him. But finally, he had a change of heart and donated valuable wood to build the vihara. The park came to be known as Jetavana Vihara after Prince Jeta's donation to the *Sangha*.

One of the most beautiful spots in Jetavana is under the Anandabodhi tree. An eternal witness to the vicissitudes of history, this sacred tree was brought as a cutting from the Bodhi tree in Anuradhapura in Sri Lanka, which itself grew from a sapling of the original Bodhi tree in Bodh Gaya.

Sudatta came to be known as Anathapindika (the incomparable alms giver). He built a magnificent, seven-storied vihara whose grandeur was commented upon by Chinese travellers several centuries later. Jetavana continues to attract pilgrims from all over the world who come here to pray and meditate in its serene atmosphere.

The ruins of Anandakuti and Gandhakuti exude an aura of sacredness because it was here that the Lord stayed during his many visits to Jetavana Vihara. In Sravasti, the Master expounded a major part of the *Tripitakas*.

It was also in Sravasti that the Lord performed the only miracle of his life in response to a challenge from six non-believers. The Lord levitated on a thousand petalled lotus, causing fire and water to leap out of his body and multiplied his person in the air.

The Lord on a thousand petalled lotus – the celebrated Miracle of Sravasti

All that remains of
Gandhakuti in
Jetavana Vihara

Close to Jetavana are the Sri Lankan, Chinese, Myanmarese (Burmese) and Thai monasteries and temples. Also worth seeing is the park with a large bell donated by Japanese pilgrims.

Mahet, to the north of Jetavana, was once a heavily fortified city. All that remains are two stupas known locally as Pakki Kuti and Kachchi Kuti; the latter identified as Sudatta's Stupa.

Pakki Kuti is said to be Angulimala's Stupa. Angulimala (literally, necklace of fingers) was a dreaded dacoit who wore a necklace of fingers that were chopped from his victims. One day in a fit of brutal rage he tried to kill his own mother. It was at this moment that the Lord met Anguliumala and Sakyamuni's enlightening words had a calming effect on his stone heart. Angulimala decided to give up his evil ways and follow the path of the Lord.

Less than a kilometre away are the ruins of a medieval Jain temple, revered by the Jains as the birthplace of the third Jain Tirthankara, Swayambunatha.

Angulimala sheds his evil past as the Lord Buddha's wise counsel prevails

GETTING THERE

By Road	Lucknow via Bahraich, 151 kms
	Kapilavastu via Naugarh, 147 kms
	Varanasi via Lucknow, 401 kms
Nearest Railhead	Balrampur, 19 kms
Nearest Airport	Lucknow, 151 kms

EXCURSIONS

A panel from Bharhut showing the Buddha's descent from heaven

Sankissa is identified with the present village of Basantpur in Farrukhabad district of Uttar Pradesh. Situated on the banks of river Kali, Sankissa is most easily accessible from Agra which is 175 kms away on the Agra-Mainpuri road. The nearest railhead is Pakhna which is 11.5 kms away.

Sankissa is the place where the Buddha descended from heaven along with Lord Brahma and Devraj Indra after giving a discourse to his mother, Mayadevi. Emperor Ashoka erected a pillar with an elephant capital to mark this holy spot.

Pleasant is Vaishali, said the Buddha to Ananda,
pleasant are its shrines and gardens.

1 Tourist Bungalow &
   Information Office
2 Garh of King Vishala
3 Abhishek Pushkarini
4 Site Museum
5 Vishwa Shanti Stupa
6 Relic Stupa
7 Ashoka Pillar
8 Amvara
   (Amrapali's village)

VAISHALI

Five years after the Enlightenment in Bodh Gaya, Lord Buddha came to Vaishali, the capital of one of the first republican states in the world. Situated on the northern banks of the Ganga, Vaishali is bound by the hills of Nepal on the north and the river Gandak on the west.

The Lichchavi nobility came to receive the Enlightened One with a cavalcade of elephants and chariots bedecked with gold. As the Lord set foot on the soil of Vaishali, loud thunder followed by a heavy downpour purged the plague-infected city. The Buddha preached the Ratna Sutra to those assembled, and eightyfour thousand people embraced the new faith.

In Vaishali for the first time women were ordained into the *Sangha*. The Buddha's foster mother, Mahaprajapati Gautami, along with 500 Sakyan women made a pilgrimage by foot from Kapilavastu to Vaishali, seeking to join the Order.

Three times the Lord refused their entreaties. Ultimately they shaved their heads, donned the orange robes and beseeched the Lord once again. The Enlightened One was finally persuaded to admit the women as *bhikshunis* or nuns.

129

Kutagarshala Vihara

Vaishali is linked to Patna, 60 kms away, by the 5.5 kms long Mahatma Gandhi Bridge across the Ganga. Leaving the crowded market place of this small district town, the metalled road leads to the village of Basarh, which the British archaeologist, Alexander Cunnigham, identified as the ancient Vaishali. There is no local transport and visitors are advised to take their own vehicles for sightseeing.

Kutagarshala Vihara is 3 kms from the main town. It was built by the Lichchavis for Sakyamuni. Known as Buddha Stupa 2, this site has revealed extensive remains of a monastery with an open courtyard and a verandah. A large tank and the Kutagarshala Chaitya can be seen in the south.

It was at Kutagarshala Vihara that a monkey took the Lord's alms bowl and climbed a tree to gather honey for him. The Buddha accepted his humble offering and the monkey in great joy, leaping from tree to tree, accidentally fell and was impaled on the stump of a tree. Dying a noble death, the monkey went to heaven.

The lion on top of the 11 metre tall Ashoka pillar faces the north towards Kushinagar

Among the precious archaeological finds is the relic casket containing the ashes of the Buddha now preserved in the Patna Museum. In the north is the Ashoka Pillar with a bell capital and a large brick stupa, originally built by the Emperor to mark the site where Buddha delivered his last discourse.

Kutagarshala Vihara is open daily from 9 am to 5 pm. Entry fee is Rs. 2 per person.

1st century BC gateway panel from the Great Stupa at Sanchi illustrating the monkey's gift to the Buddha.

It was also at Vaishali that Amrapali, the famous courtesan, earned the respect of the *Sangha* and a place in history, with her generous donations. The neighbouring village of Amvara is said to be the site of Amrapali's mango grove. Once when the Lord was visiting Vaishali, Amrapali invited him to her house and the Lord graciously accepted the offer. An overjoyed Amrapali, returning on her chariot, raised a cloud of dust. The Lichchavi princes going to meet the Buddha got enveloped in the dust and learnt of the Buddha's forthcoming visit to her house.

The Lichchavi princes wanted to exchange Amrapali's honour for one hundred thousand gold coins. Amrapali steadfastly refused their offer and after the Buddha's visit to her house she was purged of all impurities. She gifted her mango grove to the *Sangha*. Amrapali joined the Order after realising the transitory nature of all things, including beauty.

> *Sweet was my singing*
> *Like the cuckoo in the grove*
> *Now my voice cracks and falters*
> *Hear it these words are true.*

Amrapali *Therigatha*

Vaishali is also renowned as the place where the Buddha delivered his last sermon. Following a severe illness, the Master asked Ananda to assemble all the *bhikshu*s. The Enlightened One told the gathering that the *Mahaparinirvana* (final extinction) was imminent. The Great Master asked the monks to spread the *Dharma* in order to bring about the good and happiness of many.

> *Bahu jana hitaya*
> *Bahu jana sukhaya.*

Going back to the town, a little way off the main road, can be seen the ruins of the mythical King Vishala's fort, from which Vaishali derived its name. Vaishali also finds mention in the Hindu epic, *Ramayana*.

A kilometre away is Abhishek Pushkarini, the coronation tank. The sacred waters of the tank anointed the elected representatives of Vaishali. Next to it stands the Japanese temple and the Vishwa Shanti Stupa (World Peace Pagoda) built by the Nipponzan Myohoji sect of Japan. A small part of the Buddha's relics found in Vaishali have been enshrined in the foundation and in the *chhatra* of the Stupa.

Relic Stupa where the Lichchavis enshrined their share of the remains of the Buddha

Near the coronation tank is Stupa 1 or the Relic Stupa. Here the Lichchavis reverentially encased one of the eight portions of the Master's relics, which they received after the *Mahaparinirvana*.

In the north is the Site Museum. It has an excellent collection dating from 3rd century BC to 6th century AD. The terracotta monkey heads in different styles are interesting.

Open daily
9 am - 5 pm.
Closed on Fridays.
Entry is free.

Bodhisattva Avalokiteshwara, 8th-9th century, eastern India

133

Inside Vishwa Shanti Stupa

Difficult is renunciation, difficult is to delight therein.
Difficult and painful is household life. Painful is association
with unequals. Pain befalls a wanderer in samsara.
Therefore do not be a wanderer, do not be a pursuer of pain.

Dhammapada 302

After his last discourse the Awakened One set out for Kushinagar, but the Lichchavis kept following him. Buddha gave them his alms bowl but they still refused to return. The Master created an illusion of a river in spate which compelled them to go back. This site can be identified with Deora in modern Kesariya village, where Ashoka later built a stupa.

Ananda, the favourite disciple of the Buddha, attained *Nirvana* in the midst of the Ganga outside Vaishali.

A hundred years after the *Mahaparinirvana*, the second Buddhist Council was held in Vaishali. The momentous results of this Council were the dispatch of missionaries to different parts of the world for the propagation of the *Dharma*.

GETTING THERE

By Road	Patna, 56 kms
	Muzaffarpur, 36 kms
	Hajipur, 35 kms
Nearest Railhead	Hajipur, 35 kms,
	on the North Eastern Railway
Nearest Airport	Patna, 56 kms

How transient are all component beings!
Growth is the nature and decay:
They are produced, they are dissolved again:
And then is best, - when they have sunk to rest.

Mahasudarshana Jataka

KUSHINAGAR

Kushinagar is the place that the Buddha chose for his *Mahaparinirvana*, or final exit from this earth. Kushinagar or Kushinara as it was then known, was the capital of the Malla republic, one of the republican states of northern India during the 6th and 5th centuries BC. Kushinagar is identified with the modern village of Kasia, 51 kms from Gorakhpur city, in eastern Uttar Pradesh.

During his lifetime the Master traversed the dusty plains of the Ganga valley, subsisting on whatever he collected as alms, and pausing to rest only during the rainy season. In 543 BC on the full moon night of *Magh* (January-February), the Master lectured to the *Sangha* at the village, Beluva, near Vaishali, on the impermanence of all living things, and said that his own life on earth was soon to end.

The Buddha in the Parinirvana posture

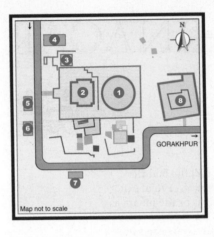

1 Main Stupa
2 Mahaparinirvana
   Temple
3 Burmese Temple &
   Monastery
4 Chinese Temple &
   Monastery
5 Archaeological Survey
   of India Office
6 Hotel Pathik Niwas
7 Mathakuar Shrine
8 Rambhar Stupa

From Vaishali the Lord went to Pava, where a
humble metalsmith, Chunda, invited the
Sangha for a meal. Having tasted the food, the
Master immediately realised that there was
something wrong with it and asked Chunda
to bury the rest so that others would not be
harmed by it. Chunda was overcome with
grief and guilt when he realised that his
offering was the cause of the Master's fatal
illness. But the Buddha consoled him saying
that the one who donates the Buddha's last
meal acquires great merit.

The Buddha desired to leave his corporeal
body at the Sal grove on the banks of the
Hiranyavati river in Kushinagar. The Master
asked the *Sangha*, whether anyone had any
queries. Sakyamuni then uttered the last
words,
*Now, bhikshus, I declare to you: all conditioned
things are of a nature to decay - strive on
untiringly.*

On a bed which Ananda had prepared under
two Sal (*shorea robusta*) trees, the Lord entered
the sphere of No Nothingness, then the sphere
of Infinite Consciousness, then the sphere of
Neither Perception, nor Non-Perception.

> *The great, wise, and most compassionate Sage converted
> everyone to the eternal Dharma and Vinaya -
> gods, men, asuras, yakshas and nagas.*

Ashokavadana 2nd century AD

King and commoner, villager and townsman, from far and near, flocked to pay obeisance to the earthly remains of the Lord for the next six days. On the seventh day the Lord's person was bedecked with garlands and taken in a procession, to the accompaniment of music. The revered *bhikshu*, Mahakashyapa, lit the funeral pyre at Mukutabandha Vihara (Rambhar Stupa) in Kushinagar. Today not much remains of this stupa except a large brick mound rising to a height of almost 15 metres set within a well-kept park.

Thereafter there ensued a war among eight great powers of north India for the possession of the holy relics. Finally the sacred relics were divided and encased in eight stupas in different parts of the country.

A solitary monk at the Rambhar Stupa where a portion of the ashes were encased

The Mahaparinirvana Temple

139

In 7th century AD, the Chinese traveller Hiuen Tsang lamented on the desolation of this sacred site. However he mentions the Mahaparinirvana Stupa. Thereafter Kushinagar sank into near oblivion, almost forgotten by the world until early this century.

The Mahaparinirvana Temple enshrines a 6 metre long statue of the Buddha in the *Parinirvana* posture. Carved from black stone, the statue now looks metallic gold because of the application of gold leaves by pilgrims.

The best time to visit this temple is in the early hours of the evening, when the mellow light from the candles and the chanting of *mantras* render a sacred aura to the temple.

Paying obeisance to the Lord in the Mahaparinirvana Temple

About 366 metres from the Mahaparinirvana Temple is the small Mathakuar shrine, built on the spot where the Buddha delivered his last sermon. Here there is a black stone image of the Buddha in the *bhumisparsha mudra* built in the 5th century AD.

There are several new monasteries and temples. The Sri Lanka - Japan monastery has an *Ashta Dhatu* (eight metals) statue of the Buddha flanked by Japanese - style portraits of his ten principal *bhikshus*. The oldest monastery in Kushinagar is the large Burmese Chandramani Bhikshu Dharamasala which is next to the Chinese Temple with its marble images of the Buddha and the White Tara.

A slender image of the Buddha in the Mathakuar shrine

Next to the meditation centre of the Sri Lanka Japanese Foundation is the new Kushinagar Museum.

Chinese Temple at Kushinagar

GETTING THERE

By Road	Gorakhpur, 51 kms
	Lumbini via Gorakhpur, 176 kms
	Kapilavastu, 148 kms
Nearest Railhead	Gorakhpur, 51 kms
Nearest Airport	Varanasi, 280 kms

SANCHI

The massive stupa at Sanchi with its intricately carved *toranas* (gateways) is noted to be the most complete example of the early Buddhist stupa in its extant form. The gateways are a masterpiece of both architecture and sculpture. Pali literary sources speak of Emperor Ashoka's dedication to the original stupa, and his erecting a pillar with a lion capital here. Sanchi was once situated on the major north-south trade route, the famous *Dakshinapatha*, and this was one of the reasons why kings and merchants continued to patronise it till well into the 6th century AD.

The Jataka stories about the Buddha's earlier incarnations form the main subject matter in the sculpted architraves. They present a fascinating array of complex images narrated in a linear fashion. The profusion of images at Sanchi seems to exude life at its fullest, reflecting the agrarian prosperity of the times (2nd century BC to 7th century AD) when Sanchi was at the height of its glory. The figure of a *yakshi* reaching out for a branch as shown in the corner of an architrave is one of the most captivating images of Sanchi.

Sanchi Museum has a small collection of sculptures from the site (caskets, pottery, parts of the gateway) of which the Ashoka lion capital, a *yakshi* and a beautiful Buddha in red sandstone are noteworthy.

(Museum is open 10 am - 5 pm daily. Closed Monday. An entry ticket of Rs 5 covers both the archaeological site and the Museum.)

Few people stay overnight in Sanchi, as the tour can be comfortably completed in one day from Bhopal, 46 kms away. Bhopal, the capital of the Indian state of Madhya Pradesh, is well connected by air and rail to Delhi, Mumbai and Chennai. Sanchi lies on the rail route between Delhi and Bhopal, and there is regular bus service from Sanchi to Bhopal.

1 Sanchi
2 Ajanta & Ellora
3 Nagarjunakonda
4 Orissa sites
5 Tawang
6 Rumtek
7 Leh
8 Dharamsala
9 Tabo

The Ajanta Caves

AJANTA & ELLORA

Situated in Aurangabad district of Maharashtra, Ajanta has acquired world renown for its famed paintings. The caves of Ajanta provided the canvas for innumerable paintings, not by Buddhist monks as commonly believed, but by highly trained members of guilds of artists under monastic and royal patronage.

Beginning in the 2nd century BC, and continuing for 900 years, twentysix caves were chipped out of a horseshoe shaped cliff. The paintings at Ajanta flow into one another, forming an endless kaleidoscope of colour and motion. Although the Jataka tales form the main theme of the paintings, also depicted are scenes from contemporary courtly life. The large individual figures painted with an eye for colour and detail, attract attention. In the Ajanta paintings we see the brilliant union between sacred and secular art. The best paintings are in cave numbers 1, 2, 16, 17 and 19; and the best sculptures are in cave numbers 4, 17, 19 and 26.

A visit to Ajanta is incomplete without visiting the nearby caves at Ellora. Starting from the 7th century AD, Ellora carried on the great legacy of Ajanta and was subject to Buddhist and later Hindu and Jain influences. The sculptures at Ellora are massive in form though they continue to reflect the fluidity of the Ajanta sculptures. There are twelve Buddhist caves in all and the entire spectrum of carvings pulsates with life and energy. The famous rock-cut Hindu temple of Kailasanath is in Ellora.

Aurangabad provides a base for visiting the caves of Ajanta, 100 kms and Ellora 30 kms away. Indian Airlines connects Aurangabad with Mumbai and Delhi.

The Ellora Cave complex

NAGARJUNAKONDA & AMARAVATI

Buddhist religion spread to Sri Lanka and Burma from the bustling Bay of Bengal ports of the Andhra coast. One of India's richest Buddhist sites, Nagarjunakonda, ancient Sri Parvata, now lies almost entirely under the Nagarjunasagar Dam. The monasteries and chaityas were reconstructed on top of a hill called Nagarjunakonda (*konda* is the Telegu word for hill), which rises from the middle of the lake. The island takes its name from the Buddhist monk, Nagarjuna, who lived around the turn of the 2nd century AD and was the exponent of the philosophy of *sunyata* (void). Statues, friezes, coins and jewellery found at the site are housed in a museum on the island and give a fascinating insight into the daily lives of this ancient Buddhist centre.

Nagarjunakonda is about 150 kms southeast of Hyderabad, the state capital of Andhra Pradesh. There is a regular ferry service to Nagarjunakonda.

Amaravati, ancient Dhanyakataka, is about 38 kms from Vijaywada, and can also be reached via Guntur, 35 kms away. An emissary of Emperor Ashoka, who went to propagate Buddhism in the region, laid the foundation of the Great Stupa at Amaravati. It has a brick-built circular *vedica* (drum) and platforms projecting in the four cardinal directions. Much of the vast archaeological findings from the site, magnificent sculpted friezes, medallions and railings, are now exhibited in the British Museum, London, and the National Museum, Delhi.

There is also a small Archaeological Museum on the site containing some of the finds from the area. Some of the exhibits are from other sites in the Krishna valley region as well.

Bodhisattava,
Ratnagiri, Orissa

ORISSA SITES

The Buddhist heritage in Orissa, though not as popular in the tourist circuit, is remarkable for its architectural wealth. The Kalinga war, which transformed Emperor Ashoka into a devout Buddhist was fought on the banks of the river Daya near the temple city of Bhubaneshwar, the capital of Orissa. Bhubaneshwar is well-connected by rail and road to the rest of the country.

Ashoka's rock edicts, dating from 260 BC, at Dhauli, 8 kms from Bhubaneshwar, stand testimony to his conversion to the gentle faith of the Buddha. These two 'Kalinga Edicts' differ from other Ashoka edicts which expound Buddhist principles. Dating from 260 BC the Dhauli edicts give detailed instructions to Ashoka's administratiors to rule his subjects with gentleness and fairness.

Six kilometres from Bhubaneshwar are the caves of Udayagiri and Khandagiri, dating from 2nd century BC, on two separate hillocks separated by a road. At Udayagiri is the famous Hati Gumpha (elephant cave) of King Kharavela. There are several caves worth visiting with stone figures from the Buddhist pantheon and fine wall friezes.

The three sites of Ratnagiri, Udaigiri and Lalitagiri, constitute a separate circuit, well-connected by road to Bhubaneshwar. Ratnagiri in the fertile Birupa river valley, 90 kms from Bubaneshwar, was a great centre of Vajrayana Buddhism till the 12th century

Buddha head, Orissa

and the Mahavihara of Ratnagiri played a great role in the development of the *Kalachakratantra* during the 10th century. Today, pilgrims can see the remains of this monastic university along with the beautiful sculpted panels that reveal the intricate motifs on the niches.

In Udaigiri, 5 kms from Ratnagiri, the remains of a sprawling monastery has been recently excavated, that can be reached through a long stairway. Rock-cut sculptures adorn the hilltop.

Lalitagiri is situated on a small hill and has a large number of votive stupas and the remains of a chaitya hall. Also noteworthy are the large number of Buddha figures housed in the Site Museum. There is a stonecarvers' village that has survived from ancient times where excellent sculptures are often to be found.

Tawang monastery

TAWANG

Tawang monastery, situated at a height of 3400 metres, in the far west of the northeast Indian state of Arunachal Pradesh, is one of the largest monasteries in India. The present monastery was built at the site of an ancient monastery in the 17th century. The VIth Dalai Lama was born near here. Tawang stands isolated from the rest of the world with its community of 500 lamas peacefully performing their daily rituals. Though difficult to reach, Tawang continues to attract scholars and pilgrims.

The main attractions are a gigantic 10 metre gilded statue of the Buddha, the large collection of priceless manuscripts, books and *tangkhas*, which depict the Buddha and tutelary deities in different poses. Indians need an Inner Line Permit and foreigners a Restricted Area Permit. Both are easily available from the Office of the Resident Commissioner, Arunachal Pradesh, New Delhi, Ph 3013956, or from FRRO offices in any of the metros. Tezpur, 216 kms away, is the nearest airport.

RUMTEK & PEMAGYANTSE

Situated in the lap of the Himalayas, the eastern Indian state of Sikkim, is famous for its gompas and their fascinating monastic ceremonies.

Rumtek monastery is visible from the capital Gangtok though it is 24 kms away in one of the lower valleys. Rumtek is the seat of His Holiness, the XVIth Gyawla Karmapa, the head of the Karma Kagyu Order of Tibetan Buddhism. On the 28th and 29th day of the tenth lunar month (July) the *cham* dance is performed by monks wearing grotesque masks and colourful dresses, culminating in a ritual dismembering of an effigy symbolising evil.

A full day's trip by car from Gangtok, the monastery at Pemagyantse (the perfect sublime lotus) is 140 kms west of Gangtok. Situated at an altitude of 2085 metres, Pemagyantse presents a panoramic view of the high Himalayas. Legend has it that the great tantric saint, Padmasambhava or Guru Rinpoche, searching for a place to meditate, shot an arrow in the air. The place where the arrow landed is where Pemagyantse monastery stands. The monastery houses on its top floor a wooden, intricately crafted structure, depicting Guru Rinpoche's abode. The annual *cham* festival is held in February.

The nearest airport is at Bagdogra, 124 kms from Gangtok, and the nearest railway stations are at Siliguri, 114 kms, and New Jalpaiguri, 126 kms from Gangtok.

Above: Rumtek monastery

Monastic ceremony in progress at Rumtek

DHARAMSALA

Upper Dharamsala or McLeodganj is in Kangra district of Himachal Pradesh. This hill station with its magnificent view of the Dhauladhar range of the Himalayas is the seat of His Holiness, the XIVth Dalai Lama and the headquarters of the Tibetan government-in-exile. The town has a large Tibetan refugee settlement. The numerous monks in their flowing maroon robes, the many streetside shops selling *momos* and butter tea, and old Tibetan women in their traditional clothes walking past serenely turning their prayer wheels, could well be in Tibet. The bazaar has shops selling Tibetan exotica. The main road leads to the Dalai Lama's temple, Namgyal monastery. It houses giant stucco statues of the Buddha, Avalokiteshwara and Padmasambhava, and the traveller can join the devout in their ritual of circumambulating the temple and rotating the prayer wheels.

Stucco image of Padmasambhava (Guru Rinpoche) in Namgyal monastery, Dharamsala

A further twenty minute trek leads to Gangchen Kyishong, where the offices of the Tibetan government-in-exile and the Library of Tibetan Works and Archives are located.

Within the same complex is the beautiful monastery of the Nechung Oracle where one can witness daily services. A stone's throw away is the Men-tsee-khang, the Centre for Tibetan Medicine. A 14 kms drive down is the Norbulingka Institute, famed for keeping the cultural life of Tibet alive.

Dharamsala is well connected by road to Pathankot (90 kms), Chandigarh (248 kms), Manali (253 kms), and Simla (317 kms). There are daily buses to Delhi (521 kms) as well. From the railway station at Pathankot there are overnight trains to Delhi. Consult your travel agent if you are planning to book a flight from the nearest airport at Gaggal (13 kms).

TABO

A mural from Tabo monastery

Tabo is located at a height of 3050 metres in the magnificently isolated Spiti valley in Himachal Pradesh. Founded in 996 AD by the great scholar, Rinchen Zangpo, as an institution for advanced learning, Tabo celebrated its 1000th anniversary in 1996. Unlike most other monasteries in the Western Himalayas, Tabo stands on barren, flat ground and is built with mud brick.

A small community of sixty monks resides here. The monastery has some rare *tangkhas* and clay statues of the Buddha painted in the Kashmiri style.

Tabo has survived because of its isolation, protected from invaders by hostile, inaccessible passes. Even today, bad weather permits trekking for only a limited period in the year. However, the small town is rapidly being modernised with electric lights and paved streets. The local shops stock basic provision for trekkers. Seasonal access by road to Manali and to Simla via National Highway 22 and State Highway30 is possible. A bus journey from Kaza, the headquarters of Spiti district, to Simla, takes two days and to Manali, twelve hours. Tabo is 33 kms, and a slow two-hour drive by bus from Kaza.

Tabo monastery, one of the oldest in the Himalayan region

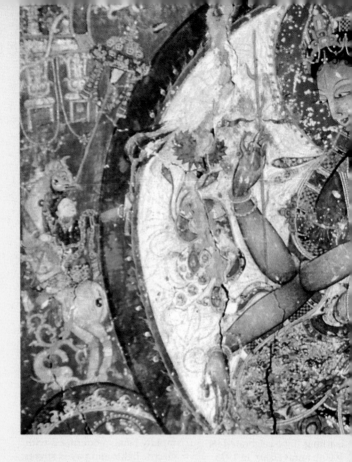

LEH

Surrounded by the snow-covered Himalayas, even the summer months, between June and September, can be quite chilly in Leh, the remote headquarters of Ladakh district, situated at an altitude of 3500 metres.

The famous Buddhist gompas (monasteries) are perched perilously on the precipices with enchanting but forbidding mountains in the background. Hemis, the largest of these gompas, founded in the 17th century, has an excellent library and is famous for housing the largest *tangkha* in India. Hemis is the most accessible of all the Ladakhi gompas and visitors flock here during the annual festival held in June-July.

Other gompas like Shey (15 kms from Leh), Spituk (8 kms from Leh), Thikse (17 kms south of Leh) are also easily accessible. However, their annual festivals are held during the winter months.

Stok Gompa and the Stok Palace Museum (10 kms south of Leh) are musts for visitors to Leh because of the rare collection of paintings and *tangkhas*. Alchi has one of the most beautiful monasteries in the Himalayan region and the 70 kms road journey from Leh is well worth the effort. Rinchen Zangpo founded Alchi Gompa in the 11th century and has some beautiful mural paintings dating from that period.

Goddess Tara, detail from a mural in Alchi monastery

Inner Line Permit, available easily from the District Commissioner's office in Leh, is required by both foreign and Indian travellers to visit the newly opened areas of the Nubra Valley, Tso Moriri and Pangong Tso.

There are daily flights by Indian Airlines to Leh from Srinagar and Delhi, but inclement weather often leads to erratic schedules. The overland routes, probably some of the most ruggedly beautiful journeys, are from Srinagar and Manali. However these roads are open only from June to October. The best season to visit Leh is between mid-May and September.

THICH NHAT HANH (born 1926)

A rare combination of mystic, poet, scholar and activist, Vietnamese Zen master Thich Nhat Hanh is one of the most beloved Buddhist teachers in the world today.

He was born in central Vietnam in 1926, and started his training under Thich Chan That of the Dhyana school of Buddhism.

As a novitiate Thich Nhat Hanh was concerned with the fact that no contemporary literature was allowed in the monastery. The young monk's request to study contemporary writings to better serve the people living in the modern world was denied. Thich Nhat Hanh and five other monks felt it best to leave the monastery. Forewarned, no other monastery accepted them. Undaunted Thich Nhat Hanh, or Thay (the Vietnamese word for teacher) as he is affectionately called, found an abandoned temple and studied the *sutras* on his own.

When he was not quite twenty years old, Thay published a book *Buddhism for Today*. He gained a reputation for being an erudite and a progressive thinker. In 1961-3, Thich Nhat Hanh studied comparative religion at Princeton and Columbia Universities in USA and was appointed lecturer of

graduate studies in Buddhism in Columbia University.

The monks who earlier turned down his request to revamp the syllabus now invited him to modernise the curriculum. For this purpose he returned to Vietnam and founded the Van Hanh University in Saigon in 1964. In the same year Thich Nhat Hanh also founded the School of Youth for Social Services (SYSS), an organisation which established schools and health clinics in Vietnam. He helped set up the La Boi Press which was to become one of the most prestigious publishing houses in Vietnam. His articles and books increasingly called for reconciliation between the warring parties in Vietnam and were censored both in South and North Vietnam.

Unfortunately, Thich Nhat Hanh's work for reconciliation resulted in his being exiled from Vietnam by both the communist and anti-communist govern-ments. Refused permission to return to Vietnam, he set up a community in France called Sweet Potatoes. After some years the Sweet Potatoes Community moved to a new retreat centre called Plum Village in southwest France. This is where Thay now lives with an ever-growing community of practitioners offering spiritual transformation to thousands of visitors each year. He also leads regular retreats around the world, including India and China, besides the USA and Europe, for families, psychotherapists, children and even for veterans of the Vietnam war.

Thich Nhat Hanh's Engaged Buddhism movement intertwines traditional meditative practices with peaceful social action. It is Buddhism in everyday life, in the midst of society, not just in a retreat centre. The idea is to find ways to speak out and work effectively. His mindfulness teachings include contemporary forms such as telephone, walking and driving meditation. Through the practice of meditation in everyday life, and by showing compassion to all living beings, our family, our entire society, will benefit.

Thich Nhat Hanh's teaching is based on conscious breathing and being fully aware of the present moment, the only moment in which we really live and in which joy is possible. This allows us to discover that *There is no way to happiness-happiness is the way*. Instead of always dwelling on what is wrong, he suggests that we meditate on what is refreshing, healing and wonderful in the present moment. "Basic peace

work is learning to develop the capacity to enjoy the peace that is already available, like breathing and enjoying fresh, clean air. If you enjoy clean air, you know that it is precious, and you will do something to prevent it from becoming unclean."

Breath is the anchor that links the mind and body in the present moment and opens the doors of wisdom and freedom. It allows for the direct experience of non-differentiation of subject and object, of interdependence, impermanence, deep compassion and deathlessness.

Thich Nhat Hanh has explained his practice in many books, including *The Heart of the Buddha's Teaching*, *Being Peace*, *The Miracle of Mindfulness*, *Living Buddha Living Christ*, and *Peace is Every Step*.

HIS HOLINESS THE XIVTH DALAI LAMA (born 1935)

Tenzin Gyatso, His Holiness, the XIVth Dalai Lama, was recognised at the age of two as the reincarnation of the previous Dalai Lama. Dalai Lamas are said to be the successive reincarnations of Avalokiteshwara, the Bodhisattva of compassion (Tibetan, *chenrezi*).

Enthroned at the age of five, the XIVth Dalai Lama assumed temporal power in 1951 but had to flee to India in 1959 along with 80,000 refugees after the Chinese occupation of Tibet. His Holiness is based at Dharamsala, Himachal Pradesh, where he heads the Tibetan government-in-exile and is recognised as spiritual and temporal leader of Tibet.

Since 1959 he has been campaigning for the peaceful return of Tibet to independence, for which he was awarded the Nobel Peace Prize in 1989.

His Holiness conducts a wide range of teaching activities, giving discourses on Buddhist texts to large audiences in Dharamsala, Bodh Gaya and other places in India.
He travels frequently around the world to speak on Buddhism and world peace. He has studied extensively all the traditions of Tibetan Buddhism. His published works include *My Land and My People*, *Freedom in Exile*, *A Human Approach to World Peace*, *The Power of Compassion* and *The Kalachakra Tantra*.

In an exclusive interview to the **Eicher Team** on 23rd February, 1999, His Holiness gave valuable insights on the *Dharma Yatra* (pilgrimage) and other facets of Buddhism.

Question: To the lay Buddhist, the *Dharma Yatra* to the sacred sites is the ultimate expression of Faith. Could Your Holiness shed more light on the *Dharma Yatra* and its significance?

Answer: *Dharma Yatra* is very important for Buddhists. When we visit these sacred sites, we are reminded of the Master, Lord Buddha. It develops in us a strong sense of compassion. Ideally, one should be a better person when one returns, otherwise it is not useful, a waste of money and time.

Question: What in Your Holiness' opinion is the enduring message of the Buddha?

Answer: The message of *ahimsa*, based on compassion. *Ahimsa* does not mean that you simply refrain from violence. People who are indifferent cannot be considered as practising *ahimsa*. *Ahimsa* implies a conscious decision to not engage in violence because of a sense of compassion and restraint. The Buddha emphasised on *karuna* (compassion).

Question: Please tell us about *Ahimsa* as a practical concept in day-to-day life, particularly how to deal with anger when confronted with violence?

Answer: As a practitioner of Buddhism, I see anger, attachment, jealousy, fear, etc. as afflictive emotions. Not just anger, this whole category of negative emotions is called *Klesh*. *Klesh* is any afflictive thought or feeling. *Klesh* causes the person to feel uncomfortable, disturbed.

Emotions such as compassion are developed mainly through training and analysis based on reasoning. When you learn to be compassionate your mind will not be easily disturbed. You will also find a greater purpose in life.

According to Buddhism, *anatman* (negation of the self) is the antidote of negative emotions, *dukha*. Since negative emotions are based on self-centredness, grasping, greed, therefore the antidote is *anatman*. It is helpful to think of the transitory nature of an object which is beyond our reach.

Once we are convinced that anger and hatred are bad, it will make a difference. Though we may still be affected by anger, it will be unable to debilitate us.

We make a mistake when we consider anger as normal and violence as manly. We consider humility as abnormal, a humble person is seen to be a coward. This is wrong. I say, analyse and think. Anger is of no use to anybody. Practice patience and tolerance, take counter measures when anger sets in. These are rational and relevant practices. Train the mind gradually and it will change.

Question: Could Your Holiness spell out the agenda for inter-religious dialogue?

Answer: One major cause of conflict throughout human history is religion. If religion causes only conflict, it is better to abandon religion. Of course, religion can play a positive role in inculcating moral and ethical values, leading to a happier life. Religion can go a long way in promoting world peace and happiness.

Our purpose would be to reduce negative aspects of religion that cause conflict. We must make every effort to accept pluralism, and appreciate others' religious traditions. One religion, one philosophy, cannot possibly satisfy everyone. The only way we can live in peaceful harmony is by engaging in serious and constructive dialogue with our fellow human beings and by recognising and respecting different religions. This is the only remedy for dissent and discontent arising from inter-faith, inter-religious conflict.

There are four basic steps whereby we can develop genuine admiration and respect for other religions.

The first step would be to meet and have a dialogue with academicians and scholars of different religions. Then to meet practitioners of different religions, which I believe to be a very potent method to understanding and resolving conflict. The next step would be to make pilgrimages to sacred sites of different religious traditions. Since the early eighties I started the practice of visiting shrines of all faiths. And finally, leaders of different religions should come together periodically to exchange ideas. And this, too, has been happening. Recently under the Bodhi tree in Bodh Gaya, Christian missionaries met me along with Muslims, Jains, Hindus, Sikhs, and we sat together and prayed.

The fact is that most people are not really very serious about religion. Serious practitioners are a minority within any religious group. What we need to focus on is not religion but ethical values. We need some method to increase deeper human values, compassion, sharing, responsibility, concern. It is not necessary to have religious faith. You could be an atheist but be a nice person and imbibe secular, spiritual ethics.

Question: Today people are realising that spiritual and religious growth are as important as material progress. Could you please elaborate on this?

Answer: Spiritualism alone is not necessary for the development of man. Just as materialism alone does not signify success. Wealthy people, driven by the desire to accumulate greater wealth, realise soon enough that money alone does not give peace and mental satisfaction. With money also there is a problem, without money also there are problems.

The rich man in his mansion surrounded by slums, lives in constant fear of theft and crime. If he is a sensitive person his own prosperity will seem meaningless when he sees the misery around him. On the other hand, if he helps the slum dwellers lead a better life, by helping them materially, the rich man will have become a happier person.

Use your wealth to be a happy person. That is the answer to a balance between spiritualism and materialism. Do something good for society, develop deeper human insight. Cultivate sensitivity and engage in social action which will benefit society and eliminate fear.

Question: What is Your Holiness' message for the new millennium?

Answer: I see nothing 'new' about the millennium, it is just a monotonous continuation in the cycle of day and night, unless we work to better ourselves and eventually try to reduce negative human qualities. Only if each of us makes the effort to improve ourselves, will we emerge as better human beings, making this world a more humane and happy place for future generations.

PRACTICAL INFORMATION

When to come to India

The best time to come to India is between October and March.

During the winter months of December and January, the day temperatures anywhere in the plains of north India are around 18˚C (64˚F) and could go down to 4˚C (39˚F) at night.

The summer months of May and June are hot, and the temperature can rise as high as 46˚C (115˚F). Tar melts on the streets and the walls burn with heat, while the overhanging dust clouds seem to trap the heat.

After the scorching heat, monsoons arrive towards the end of June and the rainy season stretches till late August.

What to wear

India does not have a fixed dress code. Local dresses such as *salwar kameez* with *dupatta* is a wonderfully relaxed and easy-to-wear dress for women, as is the *kurta* and *pajama*, with sandals or leather *kolhapuri chappals*, for men. The *sari* is the most popular attire for women, while young women and girls are seen in western clothes too.

It would be sensible to wear comfortable clothes which do not attract unnecessary attention. A windcheater or a light jacket over a cardigan or a sweater should suffice in winter. Loose cotton clothes that are cool and protect the hands and legs from the heat and the dust are the best summer wear. It is advisable to wear a scarf or a hat to protect one's head from the blazing heat of an Indian summer.

Before coming to India

There are a few things you need to take care of before travelling to India.

Visa

There are three kinds of visas for tourists.

1. The 15-day single / double-entry transit visa. This visa is valid for 30 days from the date of its issue.

2. The 3-month multiple-entry visa. This visa is valid for 90 days from the date of first entry into India, which must be within 30 days from the date of its issue.

3. The 6-month multiple-entry visa. This visa is valid for 180 days from the date of its issue, not from the date of entry into India.

Time Zone

Indian Standard Time (IST) is 5 $\frac{1}{2}$ hours ahead of Greenwich Mean Time and 10 $\frac{1}{2}$ hours ahead of US Eastern Standard Time. IST is 4 $\frac{1}{2}$ hours behind Australian Eastern Standard Time, 3 $\frac{1}{2}$ hours behind Japanese Standard Time and 1 $\frac{1}{2}$ behind Thai Standard Time.

Despite its vast geographical territory, India has just one time zone, and <u>no</u> daylight saving time in summer.

Visa Extension

It is virtually impossible to get the 15-day or 3-month visa extended. Only the 6-month tourist visa can be extended. It can be quite a bother to extend it beyond a 15-day period. Avoid it unless there is an emergency.

A 15-day extension on the 6-month visa is issued by the **Foreigner's Regional Registration Office (FRRO)** at any of the four metros: **Delhi, Calcutta, Chennai, Mumbai**. The FRRO office is open on weekdays, 9.30 am to 1.30 pm and 2 pm t 4 pm. A 15-day extension is given only if confirmed air tickets are not available. No fee is charged.

- **New Delhi:** FRRO,
  Hans Bhawan,
  1st Floor, Bahadur Shah Zafar Marg
  Ph 3319781

- **Calcutta:** FRRO,
  237 AJC Bose Road
  Ph 2473300

- **Chennai:** FRRO,
  Shastri Bhawan,
  Haddows Road, Nungambakkam.
  Ph 8275424

- **Mumbai:** FRRO,
  Dr. D.N. Road, (near Police
  Commissioners Office)
  Ph 2620446

Travel Insurance

Take a travel insurance policy, covering theft and loss, before coming to India. Also buy a medical insurance.

There are several kinds of insurance policies. Make the right choice after consulting a reliable travel agent in your country.

Driving Licence

A valid International Driving Licence is necessary if you wish to drive a car or a motorcycle in India and it is advisable to g

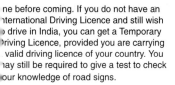

ne before coming. If you do not have an
international Driving Licence and still wish
to drive in India, you can get a Temporary
Driving Licence, provided you are carrying
a valid driving licence of your country. You
may still be required to give a test to check
your knowledge of road signs.

Health

Your health during your travel in India
depends on three things: Precautions taken
before arrival, day-to-day health care, and
efficiency in tackling emergencies.

No particular vaccination is required for
coming to India. However, visitors from
designated countries in Africa, South
America and Papua New Guinea, even if
they are on transit, are required to bring
valid Yellow Fever vaccination certificates.
In the absence of this certificate they will
be quarantined for six days.

Precautionary medication is the best bet
against common ailments like diarrhoea,
dysentery and malaria. Malaria is a problem
in India during the rainy season. So, if you
are coming at that time of the year, do
consult your doctor for precautionary anti-
malarial medication. While in India, use
mosquito repellent ointment.

If you are not already vaccinated against
hepatitis B, get it done before travelling.

Those not accustomed to Indian conditions
are usually vulnerable to stomach
problems. It is advisable to seek qualified
medical advice before travelling and carry
your own first-aid kit.

For travel health, use your common sense.
Take care of what you eat or drink. This is
the most important health rule. Water is
suspect, therefore, it is best to carry your
own mineral water. Bottled mineral water
and aerated drinks are easily avaliable and
are a good substitute for water. Hot tea and
coffee are also good alternatives.

Diarrhoea is the most common stomach
ailment. Take a three or five-day course of
anti-diarrhoea tablets duly prescribed by a
doctor.

Diarrhoea leads to dehydration. So, along
with medication, drink a lot of water with
salt and sugar. There are some restrictions
on your diet, too. Alcohol, milk, meat, fried
and spicy foods should be avoided. If the
bout of upset stomach persists, get a stool
test done because it might be amoebic
dysentery.The tropical sun is extremely
strong during the summer months, so guard
against sun stroke and dehydration. Wear a
hat and dark glasses when you go out.
Drink lots of non-alcoholic liquids, water
and fruit juice. Allow sweat to evaporate,

wear loose cotton clothes. Use sun screen
lotions and talcum powder as a precaution
against prickly heat rash.

Things you can bring into India

Visitors can bring in articles for personal
use, including cameras with 5 rolls of film,
a reasonable quantity of jewellery, a pair of
binoculars, a portable musical instrument,
a portable radio, a tape recorder, a portable
typewriter, a laptop computer and
professional equipment. On arrival, you will
have to give an undertaking on a Tourist
Baggage Re-Export (TBRE) form,
available with Customs officials at the
airport, that you will take these items back
when you leave. This form, along with the
articles that are entered in it, have to be
shown to the Customs officials at the time
of departure.

Designated 'high-value articles' are also
allowed in, but on a written undertaking
that they will be taken back at the time of
departure. Please obtain a Landing
Certificate if you are expecting
unaccompanied baggage and for
mishandled baggage.

You can bring in 200 cigarettes (or 50
cigars or 250 gms of tobacco) and liquor
and wines up to 32 oz (1 litre).

You are allowed to bring in any amount of
foreign currency in cash or travellers
cheques. However, if you are carrying more
than US $ 2500 (or equivalent), you have to
declare it on arrival. Fill up the Currency
Declaration Form (CDF) which is to be
attested by the Customs Officer. Indian
currency cannot be brought in nor taken out
of the country.

Things you can take back

Export Regulations

A visitor can take back the following goods:

(A) Souvenirs (including Indian silk, wool,
    handicrafts, etc.) without any limit.

(B) Gold jewellery and silverware up to a
    value of Rs 100,000 (and in excess of
    that only after obtaining a permit from
    the RBI, the Indian central bank).

(C) Other jewellery and precious stones,
    but if of high value, these should be
    appraised by the Customs Appraiser at
    the airport before departure. As a
    general rule, get an RBI permit for
    goods of high value.There are
    restrictions on the export of antiques
    and art objects which are more than
    100 years old. In case of doubt, consult

the Director, Antiquities,
Archaeological Survey of India
Janpath, New Delhi (Ph 3017443). It is
advisable to get a certificate of proof.
Export of most wildlife products is
either prohibited or strictly regulated.
Do not buy articles made of ivory,
reptile, tiger or deer skin, tortoise shell,
shahtoosh shawls made by killing the
Tibetan antelope.

Tax Clearance Certificate

If you stay in India for more than 120 days
(4 months), from the date of issue of the
visa, regardless of your date of entry into
India, you would be required to furnish a tax
clearance certificate to leave the country.
This is to prove that you did not earn
money while in India and that your trip was
financed with the money brought in. If you
are planning to stay in India for more than
four months, be careful with your
documents relating to travel finance.

If you are not an Indian passport
holder and you are planning to stay in India
for more than four months, apply for the
certificate at the **Income Tax Department,**
Central Revenue Building (ITO), Vikas
Marg, New Delhi. (Ph 3316161/3317828).

Foreign Travel Tax

Rs 500 has to be paid at the airport as
Foreign Travel Tax when leaving the
country. For travel to Pakistan, Nepal, Sri
Lanka, Bhutan, Myanmar, the Maldives and
Afghanistan, the tax is Rs 150.

STD CODES	
New Delhi	011
Calcutta	033
Chennai	044
Mumbai	022

Arriving in India by Air

DELHI

Delhi airport is called Indira Gandhi
International Airport. It has two terminals:
Terminal 1 (domestic) and Terminal 2
(international). The two terminals are 7 kms
away from each other. Terminal 2 is
located about 19 kms from the city centre
(Connaught Place).

You would arrive at Delhi airport to go to
north and northwestern India.

Airport Enquiry
Domestic Terminal
Ph 5655121/5665126
International Terminal
Ph 5652011/5652021

Tourist Information Offices

- **Tourist Office, Govt. of India**
  88 Janpath, New Delhi
  Ph 3320005

- **Ashok Tours & Travels (ITDC)**
  305 New Delhi House,
  Barakhamba Road
  Ph 3715917

- **Tourist Information Office**
  Govt. of UP,
  Chanderlok Bldg, 36 Janpath
  Ph 3322251/3711296

- **Tourist Information Office**
  Govt. of Bihar,
  216-216 Kanishka Shopping Plaza,
  Ashoka Road
  Ph 3368371

Airlines Offices

- **Air India**
  23 Himalaya House,
  Kasturba Gandhi Marg
  Ph 3311502
  Airport Ph 5652041/5653132

- **Indian Airlines**
  Malhotra Bldg,
  F Block, Connaught Place.
  Ph 3310517
  Airport Ph 5665121/5665313

- **Jet Airways**
  Hansalaya Bldg,
  15 Barakhamba Road
  Ph 3321317
  Airport Ph 5665404/5665875

- **Sahara India Airlines**
  Ambadeep Bldg,
  14 Kasturba Gandhi Marg
  Ph 3326851
  Airport Ph 5665234/5665875

CALCUTTA

Calcutta Airport is called Netaji Subhash
Chandra Bose Airport, and is 22 kms from
the city centre. It has two terminals,
International and Domestic, located in the
same building.

Airport Enquiry
Domestic Terminal Ph 5119637
International Terminal Ph 5118787

Airlines Offices

- **Air India**
  50 Chowringhee
  Ph 2486012/2822356
  Airport 5529685

- **Indian Airlines**
  Airlines House,
  39 Chittaranjan Ave.
  Ph 264433
  Airport 5119633

- **Jet Airways**
  Stephen Court,
  18D Park Street.
  Ph 2292660
  Airport Ph 5118836

- **Sahara India Airlines**
  Tara India Sadan,
  2A Shakespeare Sarani.
  Ph 2428969/2214910
  Airport Ph 5518357

Tourist Information Offices

- **Tourist Office, Govt. of India**
  Embassy, 4 Shakespeare Sarani
  Ph 2421402/2421475

- **Tourism Centre, Govt. of West Bengal**
  3/2 BBD Bagh East
  Ph 2488271

- **Tourist Office, Govt. of Bihar**
  Neel Kanth Bhawan, 26B Camac Street.
  Ph 2803304

- **Tourist Office, Govt. of UP**
  12-A Netaji Subhash Bose Road
  Ph 2207855

CHENNAI

Chennai airport is in Meenambakkam,
16 kms from the city centre. Both Domestic
and International Termianals are in the
same building. The Domestic Terminal is
called Kamaraj Terminal and the
international Terminal is called Arignar Anna
international Terminal.

Airport Enquiry

Domestic Terminal	Ph 2340011
International Terminal	Ph 2340551

Airlines Offices

- **Air India**
  19 Rukmani Lakshmipati Road,
  Egmore Ph 8554477
  Airport Ph 2344927

- **Indian Airlines**
  Rajah Annamalai Bldg,
  Marshall's Road Ph 8555343
  Airport Ph 2340022

- **Jet Airways**
  43/44 Montieth Road, Egmore
  Ph 8555353-57
  Airport 2346768/6557

- **Sahara India Airlines**
  4 & 5 Lokesh Towers,
  No. 18 Kodambakkam High Road
  Ph 8263661
  Airport Ph 2330056

Tourist Information Offices

- **Tourist Office, Govt. of India**
  154 Anna Salai
  Ph 8524295

- **Tourist Office, Govt. of Tamil Nadu**
  Panagal Bldg, Anna Salai, Saidapet
  Ph 4320949

- **Tourist Office, Govt. of UP**
  28 Commander-in-Chief Road
  Ph 8283276

MUMBAI

Mumbai airport, recently renamed
Chhatrapati Shivaji Airport, has two
terminals, International and Domestic.

The International Terminal is at Sahar, 29
kms from the city centre (Nariman Point).
The Domestic Terminal is 6 kms from the
International Terminal.

Airport Enquiry

Domestic Terminal	Ph 6156500
International Terminal	Ph 8366700

Airlines Offices

- **Air India**
  Air India Bldg, Nariman Point
  Ph 2024142
  Airport Ph 8366767

- **Indian Airlines**
  Air India Bldg, Nariman Point
  Ph 2023031
  Airport Ph 6114433

- **Jet Airways**
  SM Centre,
  Andheri-Kurla Road, Andheri
  Ph 8505080
  Airport Ph 6193333

- **Sahara India Airlines**
  G7 Makers Chambers,
  Nariman Point
  Ph 2831790
  Airport Ph 6119375

Tourist Information Offices

- **Tourist Office, Govt. of India**
  123 M. Karve Road
  Ph 2032932 /2033144

- **Tourist Office, Govt. of Maharashtra**
  Madame Cama Road,
  Near LIC Bldg
  Ph 2027784

- **Tourist Office, Govt. of UP**
  World Trade Centre,
  Cuffe Parade, Colaba
  Ph 2185458

STD RATES

Full rate	8 am - 7 pm
Half rate	7 pm - 8.30 pm
	7 am - 8 am
One third rate	8.30 pm - 11 pm
	6 am - 7 am
One fourth rate	11 pm - 6 am

On Sundays and national holidays, half
instead of full rate is levied during the
day.

Customs

There are two channels for customs clearance at International terminals in Indian airports: Green Channel and Red Channel.

Green Channel: This is for unhindered exit from the airport. You can walk through the Green Channel if you are not carrying goods which attract customs duty.

Red Channel: For those who have anything to declare, including money worth more than US $2500.

Transfer from Airports

Taxis: There are pre-paid taxi counters in the arrival area of all major airports. It is a good idea to hire a pre-paid taxi to avoid being over-charged.

Coaches: There are coach services for transfer into the city at most airport terminals.

Auto rickshaws: They carry up to three passengers and are cheaper than cabs. They are available outside some Indian airports though the fare may have to be negotiated.

Travel Within India

Air

There are several airlines that fly to domestic destinations. The biggest is the Indian Airlines, a state-owned domestic carrier. Other major flyers are Jet Airways and Sahara India Airlines.

Hand Baggage: In all domestic flights, passengers are allowed one piece of hand baggage. All baggage is subject to security check whether carried by hand or booked in the hold.

Baggage Allowance: Domestic airlines allow 20 kgs check-in baggage for Economy Class and 30 kgs for Business Class. Excess baggage is charged as per the schedule available at the airline's counter.

The reporting time for all domestic flights is 60 minutes prior to departure.

Onward or return reservations must be reconfirmed whenever there is a break of journey of over 72 hours. Failure to reconfirm may result in cancellation of reservation.

Tickets purchased in rupees for domestic travel are valid for one year. Tickets on the international sector, as well as those purchased with US dollars, are valid for a year from the date of journey or date of issue, as the case might be.

Indian Airlines and its subsidiary, Alliance Air, offer a 50% concession on the basic fare for senior citizens (above 65 years) and bonafide students, as does Jet Airways and Sahara India Airlines. The blind and cancer patients get a similar 50% concession from Indian Airlines. All the above concessions are available only to Indian passport holders. Indian Airlines offers a 25% concession on the basic fare to foreign students.

Indian Airlines offers two special travel packages (if paid for in US dollars).

Discover India Fare: US $500 for 15 days and US $750 for 21 days of unlimited travel with certain routing restrictions.

India Wonderfare: US $300 for 7 days of unlimited travel.

Rail

The Indian Railways run a gigantic, modern and organised network which connects the metros to most major and minor destinations within India.

Trains in India are very crowded and it is necessary to reserve a seat or a berth to travel in any degree of comfort.

Rail reservations start from 60 days before the date of travel. Reservations can be cancelled up to 24 hours before the train leaves, but a nominal cancellation fee has to be paid.

Train tickets must be bought before you enter the train. You will be penalised if you do not have one and intend to buy it on board.

International Travel Bureau on the first floor of New Delhi railway station is open Monday through Saturday, 7.30 am to 5 pm. Tickets here are issued only to foreign nationals and non-resident Indians against payment in US dollars.

Such tickets get a priority on reservation under the Foreign Tourist Quota and are exempted from reservation fees.

Indrail Passes for travel in India by train can be booked in India or abroad. The fare has to be paid in foreign currency. The passes are valid for 7 to 90 days. You can buy Indrail passes at the railway reservation offices in New Delhi and Varanasi.

Indrail Pass Prices in US $

Days	Air-cond.	1stclass	2ndclass
7	300	150	80
15	370	185	90
21	440	220	100
30	550	275	125
60	800	400	185
90	1060	530	235

Porters: All stations have a licenced porter facility. They sport a metal armband with a number on it. It is advisable to use the services of the licenced porter or *coolie*.

If you are arriving by a late night train and happen to be in an Indian railway station for the first time, railway stations are possibly the safest place to stay until morning. There are Upper Class Waiting Rooms in all stations, as well as Retiring Rooms.

Transport from the Station: Taxis and auto rickshaws are available in major railway stations. Buses are also available but they are likely to be crowded.

Getting Around

According to a recent study, there are over 5 different modes of transportation by which people manoeuvre their way around India, ranging from the latest model of the Mercedes Benz to the humble bullock cart. The level of noise in the streets of an Indian city may unnerve the first time visitor.

Auto Rickshaw: No visit to India can be complete without a ride on an auto rickshaw - a three-wheeled, black-and-yellow canopied contraption. These little vehicles are allowed to carry up to three passengers at a time. Auto rides are no joy rides, especially over bumpy roads with no discretion shown for speed. They are, however, a cheap way to travel from point to point.

Cycle Rickshaw: Cycle rickshaws are a common sight in most parts of urban and rural India.They are a convenient means of covering short distances. Not only do they precariously balance 2 to 3 people, but often carry merchandise as well.

Money

Indian Currency

Indian currency is called the Rupee. It is available in denominations of 500, 100, 50, 10, 5, 2, 1. One rupee equals 100 paise. Coins in common use are those of Rs 5, Rs 2, Re 1 and 50 and 25 paise. The 10 and 5 paise coins have become redundant in big cities, but they still have value in smaller towns and in rural India.

Tips or *Baksheesh*

There is no rule which compels you to tip anyone for any service rendered. Courtesy demands that you tip a waiter in a restaurant or hotel. The general norm is to pay 10% of the billed amount. Taxis, auto rickshaws, public transport staff, government officials or private service providers are not expected to be tipped. It is entirely up to you to tip someone for services rendered.

Sometimes the urge to tip can be misunderstood, as it may be considered an assault on personal dignity.

Credit Cards

Credit cards are becoming increasingly popular in urban areas. All major international credit cards are used, Visa, Amex, Mastercard, Diners Club.

Banks

Banks are open from 10 am to 2 pm Monday to Friday and 10 am to 12 pm Saturdays. Banks are closed on Sundays and national holidays. Most international banks have branches in major cities.

Communications

Post Offices

The main post offices in large towns provide a wide range of facilities, like telegraph, fax and a courier service which operates under the brand name EMS-Speed Post.

If you need to dispatch a letter or document urgently it might be advisable to send it by the government-run Speed Post.

Parcels by mail should not exceed 20 kgs. Books, documents, papers and printed material can be sent by book post which costs less.

All Post Offices are open from 10 am to 5:30 pm Monday to Saturday.

Telephone

ISD (international), STD (domestic long distance), and local telephone call booths are available all over India.

The rates for international calls are fixed, but calls within the country are charged on the basis of a pulse rate which varies for different cities, and for different times of the day.

Most booths remain open till midnight. Some of these booths have facilities for sending and receiving fax messages.

Emergencies

Hospitals

Indian cities have government as well as privately run hospitals and nursing homes. The government hospitals have modern medical facilities, but due to large patient turnout, medical assistance is slow.

Police Assistance Booths

Police assistance booths are located at the airports, railway stations and near the major bus stops.

Lost articles: In case of loss or theft, especially vital documents like passports, an FIR (First Information Report) must be filed at the Police Station nearest to the place where the loss occured. In case of loss of documents the embassy or high commission concerned must be immediately informed.

Phrase Book: English - Hindi

In Emergencies

help!
bachao!
stop
rukho
medicines
davai
Please call a doctor /
ambulance
*doctor / ambulance ko
bulaiye*
Where is the nearest
hospital?
*nazdeek hospital kahan
hain?*
I'm not feeling well
*Meri tabiyat theek nahin
hai*
Where is... ?
Kahan hai...?
When will... be back?
...vaapas kab ayenge?
Call the police
Police ko bulaiye

Useful Phrases

How are you?
Aap kaise hain?
Very well, thank you
*Hum theek hain,
dhanyavad.*
What is your name?
Aap ka naam kya hain?
My name is...
Mera naam...hain
See you
Phir milenge
What is the time?
Kitna baja hai?
Where are you from?
Aap kahan se aaye hain?
Do you speak English?
*Kya aap angreji bolte
hain?*

Do you have change?
Khule paise milenge?
Do you have...
Aap ke paas...hain?
How much does this cost?
Yeh kitne ka hai ?
Do you take credit cards?
Aap credit card lete hain?
I'm just looking
Main sirf dekh rahan hoon

Communication Essentials

greetings	*namaste/ namaskar*
yes	*han*
no	*nahin*
thank you	*dhanyavad/ shukriyan*
money	*paisa / rupaye*
time	*samay*
day	*din*
night	*raat*
morning	*subah*
evening	*shaam*
afternoon	*dopeher*
today	*aaj*
tomorrow	*kal*
yesterday	*kal*
here	*idhar / yahan*
there	*udhar / wahan*
food	*khana*
water	*paani*
girl	*ladki*
boy	*ladka*
woman	*aurat*
man	*aadmi*
who	*kaun*
why	*kyon*
what	*kya*
where	*kahan*
when	*kab*
how	*kaise*
one/two	*ek/do*

Shopping

What is this?	*Yeh kya hain?*
clothes	*kapda*
shoes	*joota*
big	*bara*
small	*chhota*
black	*kala*
white	*safed*
red	*lal*
blue	*neela*
yellow	*peela*
green	*hara*

Useful Words

hot	*garam*
cold	*handa*
good	*achcha*
bad	*bura*
open	*khula*
close	*bandh*
left	*baayen*
right	*daayen*
near	*paas*
far	*dur*
up	*oopar*
down	*neeche*
outside	*bahar*
inside	*andar*
fast	*jaldi*
slow	*dheere*
car	*gadi*
bus	*bus*
road	*sarak*
way	*raasta*
house	*ghar, makaan*
door	*darwaaza*
fan	*pankha*
electricity	*bijlee*
train	*train, rail gadi*
aeroplane	*hawai jahaj*

ustralia
50G Shanti Path,
anakyapuri
6888223/6885556
x 6885199

Calcutta Ph 2214618
hennai Ph 5341724
umbai Ph 2186995

ustria EP-13
handragupta Marg,
anakyapuri
6889050/ 6889049
x 6886929

Calcutta Ph 2403306
ennai Ph 8276036
umbai Ph 2072046

angladesh
Ring Road,
jpat Nagar III
6834668/6839209
x 6840596

Calcutta Ph 2475208/
-75209

elgium
N Shanti Path,
anakyapuri
608295/608067
x 6885821/604072

Calcutta Ph 2422409
ennai Ph 2352336
umbai Ph 4974302

hutan
andragupta Marg,
anakyapuri
609218/609217

Calcutta Ph 2473159

ambodia
4 Panchsheel Park
6495091/6495092
x 6495093

anada
8 Shanti Path,
anakyapuri
6876500
x 6876579

Calcutta Ph 2209281
ennai Ph 8529818
umbai Ph 2876027

hina
-D, Shanti Path,
anakyapuri
600328/600329
x 6885486

umbai Ph 4952426

enmark
Aurangzeb Road
3010900
x 3010961

Calcutta Ph 2486740
ennai Ph 8274727
umbai Ph 2618181

Finland
E-3, Nyaya Marg,
Chanakaypuri
Ph 6115258/6118096
Fax 6885380

Calcutta Ph 2474328
Chennai Ph 8523622
Mumbai Ph 38663371

France
2/50-E Shanti Path,
Chanakyapuri
Ph 6118790
Fax 6872305

Calcutta Ph 2457300
Chennai Ph 8270469
Mumbai Ph 4950918

Germany
6/ 50-G Shanti Path,
Chanakyapuri
Ph 604861/6889144
Fax 6873117

Calcutta Ph 4791141
Chennai Ph 8271747
Mumbai Ph 2832422

Greece
16 Sunder Nagar
Ph 4617800/4617854
Fax 4601363

Hungary
2/50, Neeti Marg,
Chanakyapuri
Ph 6114737
Fax 6886742

Mumbai Ph 2020224

Indonesia
50-A Kautilya Marg,
Chanakyapuri
Ph 6118642 /6118646
Fax 6884402

Calcutta Ph 2480109
Chennai Ph 2341095
Mumbai Ph 3868678

Ireland
13 Jor Bagh
Ph 4615485/4698608
Fax 4697053
Mumbai Ph 2872045

Israel
3 Aurangzeb Road
Ph 3013238
Fax 3014298

Calcutta Ph 2800028
Mumbai Ph 3862793

Italy
50-E Chandragupta Marg,
Chanakyapuri
Ph 6114355
Fax 6873889

Calcutta Ph 4792414
Mumbai Ph 3804071

Japan
50-G Shanti Path,
Chanakyapuri
Ph 6876581
Fax 6885587

Calcutta Ph 2422241
Chennai Ph 8265594
Mumbai Ph 4933857

Laos
A53, Panchsheel Park
Ph 6497447
Fax 6495812

Malaysia
50-M Satya Marg,
Chanakyapuri
Ph 601291/601292
Fax 6881538

Chennai Ph 4343048
Mumbai Ph 2660056

Mongolia
34 Golf Links
Ph 4631728
Fax 4633240

Myanmar
3/50F Nyaya Marg,
Chanakyapuri
Ph 6889007
Fax 6877942

Mauritius
5 Kautilya Marg,
Chanakyapuri
Ph 3011112
Fax 3019925

Chennai Ph 2346693
Mumbai Ph 2845466

Nepal
1 Barakhamba Road
Ph 3329218
Fax 3326857

Calcutta Ph 4791117

New Zealand
50N Nyaya Marg,
Chanakyapuri
Ph 6883170
Fax 6872317

Chennai Ph 878956

Norway
50/C Shanti Path,
Chanakyapuri
Ph 6873573/6873142
Fax 6873814

Calcutta Ph 2474757
Chennai Ph 524314
Mumbai Ph 2842098

Pakistan
2/50G Shanti Path,
Chanakyapuri
Ph 6888329/6871821
Fax 6882739

Portugal
13 Sunder Nagar
Ph 4601262
Fax 4601252

Russia
Shanti Path,
Chanakyapuri
Ph 6873799/6873800
Fax 6876823

Calcutta Ph 4797006
Chennai Ph 4982330

Singapore
E6 Chandragupta
Marg, Chanakyapuri
Ph 6885659
Fax 6886798

Calcutta Ph 2424106
Chennai Ph 8276637
Mumbai Ph 2023205

South Africa
B18 Vasant Marg,
Vasant Vihar
Ph 6119411/6119420
Fax 6113505

Calcutta Ph 2402439
Mumbai Ph 3893725

South Korea
9 Chandragupta Marg,
Chanakyapuri
Ph 4679245
Fax 6884840

Calcutta Ph 2488220
Mumbai Ph 3886743

Spain
12 Prithiviraj Road
Ph 3792085/ 3792082
Fax 3793375

Calcutta Ph 4695954
Chennai Ph 4942008
Mumbai Ph 2874797

Sri Lanka
27 Kautilya Marg,
Chanakyapuri
Ph 3010201
Fax 3015295

Calcutta Ph 2482912
Chennai Ph 8270831
Mumbai Ph 2045861/
2048303

Sweden
Nyaya Marg,
Chanakyapuri
Ph 6110735/6875760
Fax 6885401

Calcutta Ph 293639
Chennai Ph 8275792
Mumbai Ph 4360493

Switzerland
Nyaya Marg,
Chanakyapuri
Ph 604225
Fax 6873093

Calcutta Ph 2295542
Chennai Ph 4332701
Mumbai
Ph 2884563

167

Thailand	**United Kingdom**	**United States of America**	**Vietnam**
56N Nyaya Marg, Chanakyapuri Ph 605679/6118103/ 6118104 Fax 6872029	Shanti Path, Chanakyapuri Ph 6872161 Fax 6872882	Chanakyapuri Ph 6889033 Fax 4190017	17 Kautilya Marg, Chanakyapuri Ph 3018059/3012133 Fax 3017714
Calcutta Ph 4407836 Mumbai Ph 3631404	Calcutta Ph 2825171 Chennai Ph 8273136 Mumbai Ph 2830517	Calcutta Ph 2823611 Chennai Ph 8273040 Mumbai Ph 3633611	

Indian Diplomatic Missions Abroad

Australia
3-5 Moonah Place
Yarralumia
Canberra, ACT-2600
Ph (6) 273 3999
Fax (6) 2733328
25 Bligh Street,

Level 27, Sydney,
New South Wales 2000
Ph (2) 92239500
Fax (2) 92239246

Austria
Karntnerring 2,
A 1010, Vienna
Ph (1) 5058666
Fax (1) 5059219

Bangladesh
House No.120,
Road No.2, Dhanmondi
Residential Area,
Dhaka
Ph (2) 503606
Fax (2) 863662

Mundalow-2, B2 Road
No.1 Kulsi,
Chittagong
Ph (31) 619965

Belgium
217 Chaussee de
Vleurgat 1050, Brussels
Ph (2) 640 9140
Fax (2) 648 9638

Bhutan
India House Estate,
Thimpu
Ph (9752) 22162
Fax (9752) 23195

Cambodia
Villa No 777,
Boulevard Monivong,
Phnom Penh
Ph (23) 720912
Fax (23) 364489

Canada
10 Springfield Road,
Ottawa,
Ontaria-KIM 1 C9

Ph (613) 744 3751
Fax (613) 744 0913

Suite No. 500,
2 Bloor Street West,
Toronto
Ph (416) 9604831
Fax (416) 9609812
325 Howe Street,
2nd floor, Vancouver
Ph (604) 6628811
Fax (604) 6822471

China
1Ri Tan Dong Lu,
Beijing 100600
Ph (10) 5321903
Fax (10) 5324684/220

Yan Anan (West) Road,
Shanghai 200335
Ph (21) 2758885
Fax (21) 2758881

Denmark
Vangehusveg 15,
2100 Copenhegan
Ph (45) 3118 288
Fax (45) 31299201

Finland
Satamakatu,
2 A8 Helsinki 16
Ph (0) 608927
Fax (0) 6221208

France
15 Rue Alford
Dehodencq, 75016
Paris
Ph (1) 40507070
Fax (1) 40500996

Germany
Adenaueralle 262-264,
53113 Bonn 1
Ph (228) 54050
Fax (228) 540 5153

Majakowskiring 55,
13156 Berlin
Ph (30) 4853002
Fax (30) 4853003

Mittelweg 49,
60318 Frankfurt / AM
Main
Ph (69) 1530050
Fax (69) 554125

Raboisen 6,
20095 Hamburg
Ph (40) 338036
Fax (40) 323757

Indonesia
S1 Jalan H R Rasuna
Said Kunaingan
Jakarta Selatan 12950
Ph (21) 5204150
Fax (21) 5204160

Ireland
6 Leeson Park,
Dublin-6
Ph (1) 4970843
Fax (1) 4978074

Israel
4 Kaufman Steet,
Sharbat Street,
Tel Aviv 68012
Ph (3) 5101431
Fax (3) 510 1434

Italy
Via XX Settembre 5,
00187 Rome
Ph (6) 4884642
Fax (6) 4819539

Via Larg 16,
(5th& 6th floor)
20122 Milan
Ph (2) 8057691
Fax (2) 72002226

Japan
2-2-11 Kudan minami,
2 Chome, Chiyoda Ku,
Tokyo 102
Ph (3) 326 22391
Fax (3) 32344866

Osaka-Kobe Semba
I.S.Bldg, 10th Floor,
9-26 Kyutaromachi,
1Chome, Chuo-ku,
Osaka 541
Ph (6) 2617299
Fax (6) 2617799

Malaysia
No. 2 Jalan Taman
Duta,
off. Jalan Duta
P.O.Box 10059,
50480 Kuala Lampur.
Ph (603) 2533504
Fax (603) 2533507

Maldives
Athireeg, Aage,
Ameeru Ahmed, Magu,
Henvieru, Male
Ph (960) 323014
Fax (960) 324778

The Netherlands
Buitenrustweg 2,
2517 KD, The Hague
Ph (70) 3469771
Fax (70) 3617072

New Zealand
180 Molesworth Street
P.O. Box 4045,
Wellington
Ph (4) 4736390
Fax (4) 4990665

Norway
Niels Juels, Gate 30,
0244 Oslo 2
Ph (22) 443194
Fax (22) 440720

Pakistan
G5 Diplomatic Enclave
Islamabad
Ph (51) 814371
Fax (51) 820742

Portugal
Rua Pero da Covilha
16, 1400 Lisbon
Ph (1) 3017291
Fax (1) 3016576

Russian Federation
6-8 Ulitsa Vorontosov
Polye (Obukha),
Moscow
Ph (095) 9170820
Fax (095) 975233735

Ulitsa, Reyleeva,
St. Petersburg, 19112:
Ph (812) 2721731
Fax (812) 2722473

Singapore
India House,
31, Grange Road,
P.O.Box No. 912304
Ph (65) 737 6777
Fax (65) 7326909

Mauritius
Life Insurance
Corporation of India
Bldg, 6th floor,
President John
Kennedy Street,
P.O. Box 162,
Port Louis
Ph (230) 2083775
Fax (230) 2086859

Nepal
Lain Chaur,
P.O. Box 292,
Kathmandu
Ph (71) 411940
Fax (71) 413132

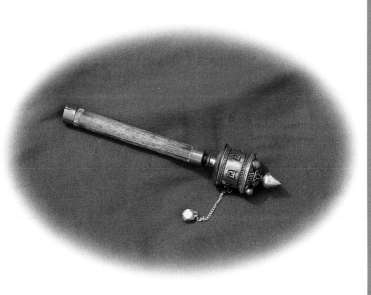

The Buddhist sites in India are located in the two states of Bihar and Uttar Pradesh. For travellers wanting to tread the path of the Buddha, the journey begins at either of the two entry points to the circuit, Patna in Bihar or Varanasi in Uttar Pradesh.

Patna, the capital of Bihar in eastern India, provides easy access to the most important centre of Buddhism, Bodh Gaya. Rajgir, Nalanda and Vaishali, the other important sites, are also easily accessible from Patna.

Varanasi, in the adjoining state of Uttar Pradesh, is only 10 kms from Sarnath, where the Buddha first preached the eternal Dharma. His birthplace, Lumbini (now in Nepal), Kushinagar, the site of his Mahaparinirvana and the sacred sites of Kapilavastu and Sravasti can also be covered.

PATNA

Arriving by Air

Patna Airport is 8 kms from the city centre (Gandhi Maidan). Patna is connected by air to Calcutta, Mumbai, New Delhi, Varanasi and Lucknow.

Domestic Airlines Offices

Indian Airlines
South of Gandhi Maidan
Ph 222554/226433 Fax 227310
Airport 231453/223199
(Alliance Air, a subsidiary of Indian Airlines, also operates from Patna).

Sahara India Airlines
2nd Floor Mona Cinema,
East of Gandhi Maidan
Ph 661109 Fax 228307
Airport 661289

(Sahara does not operate flights throughout the year. It is worthwhile checking out whether their flights are operational).

Air connections from Patna

▶ Patna-Varanasi-Delhi
   S2 521 Sahara Airlines Daily

▶ Delhi-Lucknow-Patna-Calcutta
   CD 411/412 Alliance Air Daily

▶ Mumbai-Delhi-Patna-Ranchi
   IC 809/810 Indian Airlines Daily

▶ Patna-Lucknow-Mumbai
   S2 907 Sahara Airlines Mo/We/Fr

Arriving by Train

Patna Junction Railway Station is about 2.5 kms from Gandhi Maidan. Patna is connected by train to all major cities.

Patna Railway Station has a fully computerised Reservation Centre.

Railway Enquiry Ph 131, 133, 427812-15
Reservations Ph 222197

Important Train Connections

Train Nos/ train Names

❖ New Delhi-Patna via Varanasi
   2401/2402 Shramjeevi Express

❖ New Delhi-Patna via Mughal Sarai
   2309/2310 Patna Rajdhani Exp

❖ New Delhi-Howrah
   2305/2306 Howrah Rajdhani Exp

❖ New Delhi-Patna
   2392/2391 Magadh Exp

❖ New Delhi-Howrah via Patna
   2304/2303 Poorva Exp

❖ Kurla (Mumbai)-Patna
   3202/3201 Patna-Kurla Exp

Note:
Not all the trains run daily. It is advisable t check in advance.

Travelling by Road

Patna is connected by National Highways to Calcutta and Varanasi and State Highways to all major towns in Bihar.

Important Road Distances

Bodh Gaya via Jehanabad	115 kms
Bodh Gaya via Rajgir	181 kms
Calcutta	607 kms
Nalanda	90 kms
Rajgir	100 kms
Vaishali	63 kms
Varanasi (via Mohania)	278 kms

Bus

The main bus terminus in Patna is at Bir Kunwar Singh Park (near Patna Junction Railway Station). **Enquiry Ph 221475**

har State Road Transport Corporation SRTC) buses ply to all major destinations Bihar. Services begin at daybreak and ontinue till late at night. There are several SRTC bus services to Varanasi every day. he journey takes 8-10 hours.

ar Rentals

ou can hire a private taxi for local and utstation tours through travel agencies in otels in Patna and Varanasi. The rates are pproximately Rs 4 per km for 8 hours ithin the city and Rs 5.50 per km for utstation travel. The night halt charges are pproximately Rs 100. The rates for hiring a xi at any of the sites in the Buddhist rcuit are approximately the same as ove.

ocal Transport

atna does not have any black-yellow taxis. rivate taxis are available from the Airport, ailway Station and some hotels. It is dvisable to fix rates beforehand. Auto ckshaws and cycle rickshaws are easily vailable, but with them too it is advisable fix rates beforehand.

> **Foreigner's Regional Registration Office**, Behind the Superintendent of Police Office, beside SK Memorial Hall, near Gandhi Maidan (no telephones).

ourist Information Centres

- **Bihar State Tourism Development Corporation (BSTDC)**, Birchand Patel Marg Ph 225411
- **BSTDC**, Hotel Pataliputra Ashok, Birchand Patel Marg Ph 223238/226272
- **BSTDC**, Patna Junction Railway Station Ph 221093
- **Ashoka Travels and Tours, India Tourism Development Corporation (ITDC)**, Hotel Pataliputra Ashok Ph 223238
- **Tourist Office, Govt of India**, Sudama Palace, Old By Pass Road Ph 345776

onducted Tours

har Tourism operates conducted tours om Patna to Bodh Gaya daily. Deluxe uses leave at 7 am and return the same ay. There are weekend package tours overing Bodh Gaya, Rajgir and Nalanda. he tour does not operate without a inimum of 35 bookings.

DC operates special tours on request om October to March covering the entire uddhist Circuit in AC and non AC cars and oaches. Bookings have to be made at ast 15 days in advance. A minimum oking of 5 tourists per car and 35 tourists

for coaches have to be made. The round trip covers around 1200 kms, including local sightseeing. The tour starts with Varanasi and Sarnath and then proceeds to Bodh Gaya, Rajgir, Nalanda, Patna and Vaishali.

Travel Agencies

- Ashok Travels and Tours ITDC
- Hotel Pataliputra Ashok (Govt. of India Undertaking) Ph 223238
- Travel Corporation of India, Maurya Hotel Ph 221699/232482
- Arya Travels, Maurya Hotel Complex, South of Gandhi Maidan Ph 239422
- Ma Bhagwati Travels, Buddha Colony Ph 220206
- Welcome Travels, Opposite Divisional LIC (Life Insurance Corporation), Fraser Road Ph 33571

Authorised Money Changers

- **Bank of India**, Fraser Road. Open Monday to Saturday 10 am - 2 pm. Ph 231337
- **State Bank of India**, West of Gandhi Maidan. Open Monday to Saturday 10 am - 2 pm.

Hospitals, Nursing Homes

Patna and Varanasi have several government as well as privately run hospitals and nursing homes. All government hospitals have modern medical facilities, but due to large patient turnout, medical assistance is slow. Service at the privately run hospitals and nursing homes is more efficient and assistance quicker.

- Brindavan Nursing Home, Salimpur Arha Ph 656263
- Holy Family Hospital, Kurji Digha Ph 262516/262540
- Indira Gandhi Institute of Medical Sciences, Sheikhpura Ph 287407*
- Nalanda Medical College Hospital, Old By Pass Road Ph 641159*
- Patna Medical College Hospital, Ashok Rajpath Ph 671252*
- Rajendra Memorial Research Institute, Agam Kuan Ph 641565*
- Sahyog Hospital, Pataliputra Colony Ph 265117/262642

*Government hospitals

> **Important Phone Numbers**
> Police Station, East of Gandhi Maidan
> **Ph 673519**
> Traffic Police **Ph 673999**
> Emergency/Ambulance **Ph 102**
> International Trunk Call Booking
> **Ph 225111**

Communications

- ✉ **General Post Office**, August Kranti Marg Ph 221620/224000 is open on Sundays till 8 pm.

- ✉ **Central Telegraph Office**, August Kranti Marg is open round the clock.

- ✉ **Speed Post Office**, Revenue Building, Birchand Patel Marg.

STD/ISD booths are located all over the city and are open from 7 am to 11 pm

Where to Stay

Patna has hotels in Luxury, Economy and Budget categories. Most charge 7% luxury tax and 10% service charge. Some give off-season discounts. Most of them accept all major credit cards but make sure before you check in. Most hotels in the luxury and economy categories have authorised money changers and in-house travel agencies. It is advisable to use them for travel reservations.

Luxury

(Above Rs 1500 for a standard room with single occupancy)

- ⬤ **Chanakya** Birchand Patel Marg. 6 kms from Airport. Ph 223141 Fax 220598 Centrally airconditioned.

- ⬤ **Maurya** Patna South Gandhi Maidan. 8 kms from Airport. Ph 222060-68 Fax 222069 Centrally airconditioned.

- ⬤ **Pataliputra Ashok** Birchand Patel Marg. 6 kms from Airport. Ph 226270-75 Fax 223467 Centrally airconditioned.

Economy

(Rs 750 and up to Rs 1500 for a standard room with single occupancy)

- ⬤ **Anandlok** Opposite Patna Junction Railway Station. 7 kms from Airport. Ph 239318/239337 Fax 223960

- ⬤ **Minar** Exhibition Road. 7 kms from Airport. Ph 227352/ 23541 Fax 230849

- ⬤ **Republic** Lawly's Building, Exhibition Road. 7 kms from Airport. Ph 655021-23 Fax 655024

- ⬤ **Samrat International** Fraser Road. 7 kms from Airport. Ph 220560-67 Fax 226386

- ⬤ **Satkar International** Fraser Road. 7 kms from Airport. Ph 220551/220550 Fax 220556 Centrally airconditioned.

Budget

(Less than Rs 750 for a standard room with single occupancy)

- ⬤ **Avantee** Opposite Dak Bungalow Road.7 kms from Airport. Ph 220540-49

- ⬤ **Marwari Awas Griha** Fraser Road. 7 kms from Airport. Ph 220625-34 Fax 220943

- ⬤ **Mayur** Fraser Road. 7 kms from Airport. Ph 224141-42

- ⬤ **President** Off Fraser Road. 7 kms from Airport. Ph 220600-605 Fax 230469

- ⬤ **Rajasthan** Fraser Road. 7 kms from Airport. Ph 225102-04 Fax 225104

- ⬤ **Tourist Bungalow** Kautilya Vihar Birchand Patel Marg. 6 kms from Airport. Ph 225411/ 210219 Fax 236218

Where to Eat

Most hotels have multi-cuisine restaurants often with bars. Some of the better known eateries are located in the 5-star hotels.

The other restaurants which we recommend include **Basant Vihar** in Mauryalok Complex for pure vegetarian cuisine; and **Amrapali** on Birchand Patel Marg and **Aharika** on Exhibiton Road for excellent Indian cuisine. **Ashoka** and **Hot Breads** on Fraser Road are worth trying out as is **Mayfair** on Dak Bungalow Road for snacks and ice creams.

Where to Shop

The major shopping areas around **Gandhi Maidan** are **Mauryalok**, **Hira Place**, **Birchand Patel Marg** and **Patna Market**. Shopping centres in Patna are open from 10 am to 8 pm daily and are closed on Sundays. Patna is famous for its tassar silk khadi cottons and stone ware.

STD Codes

Bodh Gaya	0631
Kushinagar	05563
Nalanda	06112
Patna	0612
Rajgir	06119
Sarnath	0542
Sonauli	05522
Sravasti	05252
Vaishali	06225
Varanasi	0542
Siddharthnagar	05544

VARANASI
(BENARAS, KASHI)

Arriving by Air

Varanasi Airport is at Babatpur, 22 kms from Varanasi Railway Station and 26 kms from the city centre at Godaulia. Varanasi is connected by air to Lucknow, Delhi, Agra, Mumbai, Khajuraho and Kathmandu.

It is advisable to hire a taxi at the Airport for transfer to the city centre, as the bus service is often erratic.

Airport Enquiry Ph 343742

Domestic Airlines Offices

Indian Airlines
2 Yadunath Marg, Cantonment.
Ph 348637/343746
Airport Ph 345959
(Alliance Air, a subsidiary of Indian Airlines, also operates from Varanasi)

Sahara India Airlines
Mint House Motel, Nadesar, Cantonment.
Ph 342355 Fax 343094
Airport Ph 622334

Jet Airways
1st Floor, Krishnayatan Building,
S 20/56 D Kennedy Road The Mall,
Cantonment. Ph 511444/511555
Airport Ph 622577/88

Air connections from Varanasi

- Varanasi-Delhi-Mumbai
  IC 805/806 Indian Airlines Daily
- Delhi-Agra-Khajuraho-Varanasi
  CD 407/408 Alliance Air Daily
- Varanasi-Kathmandu
  IC 751/752 Indian Airlines Daily
- Delhi-Varanasi-Khajuraho
  9W 723/724 Jet Airways Daily
- Delhi-Varanasi-Patna
  S2 521/522 Sahara Airlines Daily

The flights to Varanasi mainly originate in Delhi and are often subject to delays in the winter months of January and early February when Delhi Airport is often fogbound in the mornings. It is advisable to check if your flight is on time.

Arriving by Train

Varanasi Railway Station, is in the Cantonment area. 16 kms from Varanasi is another important railway station, Mughal Sarai Junction. Both these stations are well connected by the North Eastern railway to all the major cities. Both of them have fully computerised Reservation Centres. The booking office is open all days of the week from 8 am to 8 pm.

There is left-luggage facility at both Varanasi and Mughal Sarai Railway Stations. Both are open 24 hours.

**Varanasi Railway Station Enquiry
Ph 132/135**

**Mughal Sarai Junction Enquiry
Ph 925703**

Important Train Connections

Train Nos/ Train Names

- New Delhi-Varanasi
  4057/4058 Kashi Vishwanath Express
- Patna-New Delhi
  2309/2310 Patna Rajdhani Exp.
- Mumbai-Varanasi
  1065/1066 Kurla Varanasi Exp.
- Chennai-Varanasi
  6039/6040 Ganga Kaveri Exp.
- Pune-Varanasi
  1031/1032 Pune Varanasi Exp.
- Secunderabad-Varanasi
  7092/7091 Secunderabad Varanasi Exp.
- Howrah (Calcutta)-New Delhi
  2381/2382 Poorva Exp
- Howrah-New Delhi
  2301/2302 Howrah Rajdhani Exp
- Puri-New Delhi (via Mughal Sarai)
  8475/8476 Neelachal Exp.

*Not all the trains run daily. It is advisable to check in advance.

Travelling by Road

Varanasi is situated at the junction of NH2, NH7 and NH29, and is well connected by National Highways to Calcutta and Patna and by State Highways to all major towns of Uttar Pradesh.

Important Road Distances

Agra	565 kms
Allahabad	125 kms
Bodh Gaya	240 kms
(via Mohania)	
Calcutta	677 kms
Delhi	765 kms
Gorakhpur	212 kms
Kaushambi	190 kms
Kushinagar	267 kms
Lucknow	286 kms
Patna (via Mohania)	246 kms
Sarnath	10 kms
Sonauli (Nepal border)	386 kms

Bus

There are two bus stands in Varanasi, one on Sher Shah Suri Marg, in the Cantonment area and the other one is at Godoulia.

UP Roadways operates bus services from both the bus stands to Allahabad, Gorakhpur and Lucknow.

UP Roadways Enquiry Ph 342011/330740 (open 24 hours)

Private deluxe buses are also available, but it is advisable to personally check timings and fares at least a day in advance of travel.

Local Transport

Metered black-yellow taxis are not available in Varanasi. Local city buses cover most parts of Varanasi but are often very crowded and uncomfortable. Cycle rickshaws and horse-drawn carriages (tongas) are commonly used and quite convenient. It is advisable to fix rates before travel. Try to find out the going rate for the journey from local people and negotiate a fair price before starting.

Boats

The best way to enjoy Varanasi is by boat. Boats are available at most ghats. Approximate rate for hiring a small boat from Assi Ghat to Manikarnika Ghat and back is Rs 100.

Foreigners Registration Office
Srinagar Colony, Sithgiri Bagh.
Ph 351968.

Tourist Information Centres

- **Tourist Office, Govt of India**, 15B The Mall, Cantonment. Ph 346370/343744
- **Tourist Office, Govt of Bihar**, Englishiya Market, Sher Shah Suri Marg. Ph 343821
- **Tourist Office, Govt of UP**, Parade Kothi, Cantonment. Ph 343413/341162
- **Tourist Information Counter, Govt of UP**, Varanasi Rly Station. Ph 343544/346370
- **Tourist Information Counter, Govt of India**, Varanasi Airport, Babatpur Ph 343472

Travel Agencies

- Cosmic Travels and Movers, Varuna Bridge. Ph 346726
- Indian Tourism Development Corpn, Hotel Varanasi Ashok. Ph 342565
- Impac Tours, Nadesar. Ph 345781
- Sarnath Travels, Cantonment. Ph 360089
- Shashi Travels, Hotel Temple Town, Cantonment. Ph 348248
- Sita World Travels, 53 Cantonment. Ph 343121
- Surbhi Tours & Travels, Cooperative Building, Nadesar. Ph 348632
- Travel Corpn of India, Siridas Foundation, S-20, 51-5 & S20/52-4 Mall Road. Ph 346210
- Travel Bureau, Clarks Hotel. Ph 346621
- Varuna Travels, Pandey Haveli. Ph 323370

Conducted Tours

Most of the travel agencies arrange conducted tours on the Buddhist Circuit. Approved tourist guides for local sightseeing are available from Tourist Information Office, Govt. of India.

    1-4 tourists full day : Rs 350

    5-15 tourists full day : Rs 500

    16-35 tourists full day : Rs 750

Guides speaking foreign languages can be hired by paying a little extra.

Roadways Enquiry

UP Roadways Bus Stand, Sher Shah Su Marg, Cantonment. Ph 342011.

UP Roadways Bus Stand, Godaulia. Ph 330740.

Both are open 24 hours and run frequent services to Allahabad, Gorakhpur and Lucknow. Deluxe buses are also available

Authorised Money Changers

- **State Bank of India (SBI)**, near Hotel Surya, Cantonment, branch at Hotel de Paris, Hotel Clarks Varanasi and Hotel Varanasi Ashok.

  Open Monday to Friday. 10 am - 2 pm. Saturday 10 am - 12 am.

- **Indian Overseas Bank**, Lahurabir. Open Monday to Friday. 10 am - 2 pm. Saturday 10 am - 12 am.

Hospitals & Nursing Homes

- ✚ Ashirwad Nursing Home, Birdopur. Ph 560146
- ✚ Birla Hospital, Machhodari. Ph 56357
- ✚ Cancer Hospital, N.E. Railway, Lahertara. Ph 342538*
- ✚ Civil Hospital, Shivpur. Ph 382226*
- ✚ Dr. Gautam Chakravarti Orthopedic, Nursing Home, Guru Bagh. Ph 32177
- ✚ Gulab Nursing Home, Hukulganj. Ph 38579
- ✚ Hindu Seva Sadan, Chowk. Ph 352456
- ✚ Mata Anand Mai Hospital, Bhadaini. Ph 310592
- ✚ Ram Krishna Mission Hospital, Luxa Road. Ph 321727*
- ✚ Rajkiya Hospital, Shivpur. Ph 382226*
- ✚ Shiv Prasad Gupta Hospital, Kabir Chauraha. Ph 62424/333723
- ✚ Singh Medical Research Centre, Maldhiya. Ph 342644
- ✚ Sir Sunder Lal Hospital, Baranas Hindu University. Ph 316833/312542*
- ✚ Shubam Nursing Home, Chandrika Colony. Ph 561333
- ✚ The Heritage Hospital, Near Benaras Hindu University
- ✚ Uphaar Nursing Home, Mehmergunj. Ph 360370

*Government hospitals

Important Phone Numbers

Ambulance	**Ph 333723**
Fire	**Ph 322888**
Police Station	**Ph 348041**
District Magistrate	**Ph 348585**
Banaras Hindu University	**Ph 310290**
Bharat Kala Bhawan	**Ph 310045**
Foreigners' Registration Office	**Ph 351968**

Communications

- **Head Post Office**
  Bisheshwarganj and Cantonment.

- **Post Offices** are open 9.30 am to 5.30 pm and the **Telegraph Office** from 9.30 am to 4.30 pm.

There are STD and ISD booths in all localities that are open from 8 am to 11 pm.

Major courier services also operate from Varanasi:

- Blue Dart Express, C-21/4A/3, Sriram Shopping Complex, Maldahiya. Ph 357268/3589964

- DHL Worldwide Express, D 58/53-54 Shiva Complex, 1st Floor. Ph 9154361/412

Where to Stay

Varanasi has hotels in Luxury, Economy and Budget categories. Most charge an additional 5-7% luxury tax and 10% service charge. Some give off-season discounts. Most hotels listed here accept major credit cards but make sure before you check in. Hotels in the luxury and economy categories have authorised moneychangers and in-house travel agencies and have air-conditioned rooms. It is advisable to use the in-house travel agencies for travel arrangements.

The city also offers a wide range of guest houses and dharamshalas which offer basic but clean service. Varanasi Railway Station has Retiring Rooms which can be booked through the Matron-in-Charge, 1st floor, Varanasi Railway Station. The Railway Retiring Rooms are available for a maximum of 3 days against proof of train journey.

Hotels offer discounts during off-season but you must bargain for it because even in the hot summer months, when few tourists come to Varanasi, it is common for hotels to offer printed official tariff.

Luxury

(Above Rs 1500 for a standard room with single occupancy)

- **Clarks Varanasi**
  The Mall, Cantonment.
  20 kms from the Airport.
  Ph 348501/342401 Fax 348186

- **Hindustan International** C-21/3 Maldahiya. 20 kms from the Airport. Ph 351484/57075

- **Ideal Best Western** The Mall. 18 kms from the Airport Ph 348250/348252

- **Taj Ganges** Nadesar Palace Grounds, Cantonment. 22 kms from the Airport Ph 345100/342480 Fax 348067

- **Varanasi Ashok** The Mall. 22 kms from the Airport. Ph 346020/342550 Fax 348089

Economy

(Rs 750 and up to 1500 for a standard room with single occupancy)

- **De Paris** 15 The Mall, 20 kms from the Airport. Ph 343582/3/4 Fax 348520

- **Malti** C 31/3 Vidyapeeth Road. 22 kms from the Airport. Ph 351395 Fax 322161

Budget

(Less than Rs 750 for a standard room with single occupancy)

- **Barahdari** Maidagin. 22 kms from the Airport. Ph 330040 Fax 330581

- **Diamond** B-20/44-A-3 Bhelupur. 20 kms from the Airport. Ph 310696 Fax 310703

- **Ganges** View Assi Ghat. One of the best hotels in Varanasi, it overlooks the river and serves excellent home-cooked meals. 22 kms from the Airport. Ph 313218 Fax 313965

- **India** 59 Patel Nagar Cantonment. 20 kms from the Airport. Ph 342912 Fax 348327

- **Pallavi International** Hathwa Place, Chaitganj, 22 kms from the Airport. Ph 356939 Fax 322943

- **Radiant** YMCA Tourist Hostel 28A, Sampoornand Nagar, Sigra Ph 363928

- **Temple on Ganges** near Assi Ghat 22 kms from the Airport. Ph 312340 Fax 312740

- **UP Tourism Tourist Bungalow** Off Parade Kothi, G.T. Road. 20 kms from the Airport. Ph 343413

Where to Eat

Varanasi has restaurants that are varied not only in their ambience but also in their rates.

All top hotels have restaurants offering Indian, European and Chinese cuisine. Some of the better restaurants are **Canton's**, **Hotel Surya**, Cantonment and **Winfa**, Lahurabir for authentic Chinese food. **Konamey** on Dasashwamedha Raod and **El Parador** behind city bus stand for basic European food. **Tulsi** in Chaitganj and **Jalajog** in Godaulia offer excellent Indian food.

City restaurants are not allowed to serve alcohol. Hotels do not serve alcohol on 1st and 7th of each month and on certain public holidays.

Where to Shop

Varanasi is internationally famous for its silks and brocades. The visitor should also check out on Varanasi's brassware, gold jewellery, painted wooden toys and handwoven carpets. Among the main shopping areas are **Chowk**, **Dasashwamedh Road**, **Godaulia** and **Vishwanath Gali**.

Worth visiting are the handloom and handicrafts showrooms run by the State Government, **UPICA** at Nadesar and **UP Handlooms** at Lahurabir and Nadesar.

BODH GAYA

Arriving by Air

The nearest Airport is at Patna, 125 kms away. (*see*: Patna)

Arriving by Train

Gaya Railway Station is 15 kms away. Gaya is connected by train to all major Indian cities.

Important Train Connections

Train Nos/ Train Names

- New Delhi-Howrah via Mughal Sarai (MS* & Gaya) 2301/2302 Howrah Rajdhani Express
- New Delhi-Bhubaneshwar via MS & Gaya 2421/2422 Bhubaneshwar Rajdhani Express
- New Delhi-Howrah via Varanasi & Gaya 2381/2382 Poorva Exp
- Howrah-Kalka via MS & Gaya 2311/2312 Kalka Mail
- Howrah -Jodhpur via Gaya 2307/2308 Jodhpur-Howrah Exp
- Howrah-Dehradun via Varanasi & Gaya 3009/3010 Doon Exp
- Howrah-Gwalior 1159/1160 Chambal Exp
- Howrah-Mumbai via MS & Gaya 3003/3004 Howrah Mumbai Mail

Note:

Not all the trains run daily. It is advisable to check in advance.

Mughal Sarai Junction, is 16 kms from Varanasi Railway Station.

The Railway Station in Calcutta is in Howrah.

Important Phone Numbers

Bodh Gaya Police Station **Ph 400741**
Railway Enquiry Gaya **Ph 131, 20283**
Railway Reservation Gaya **Ph 22932**
Mahabodhi Mahavihara Buddhagaya
Temple Management Committee
Ph 400735 Fax 400777

Travelling by Road

Bodh Gaya is well connected by National Highways to Patna and Varanasi and by State Highways to other major towns of Bihar. It is advisable not to travel after dark.

Important Road Distances

Gaya	16 kms
Patna via Jehanabad	115 kms
Patna via Rajgir	181 kms
Rajgir	70 kms
Varanasi via Patna	393 kms

Bus

Bihar State Road Transport Corporation (BSRTC) buses operate regularly from Bodh Gaya to Patna and Varanasi. **Bihar Tourism Development Corporation** operates deluxe coach service daily to and from Bodh Gaya from its headquarters in Patna. (*see* : Patna)

Local Transport

Taxis or buses are not required for travel within Bodh Gaya. The best way to move around within Bodh Gaya is on foot since all the important sites are located within walking distance. Cycle rickshaws and tongas (horse drawn carriages) are easily available and are the most favoured mode of transport within the town. There is a regular bus service to Gaya, 15 kms away.

Tourist Information Centres

- **Tourist Information Centre, Govt of Bihar**, Mini Market, Opp. Mahabodhi Temple, Bodh Gaya Ph 400672. Open 10 am - 8 pm.
- There is a Govt of Bihar run tourist information booth at Gaya Railway Station.
- **Bihar State Tourism Development Corporation**, Hotel Siddhartha Vihar, Bodh Gaya Ph 400445

Some tourist literature is also available at the main gate, Information Office of the Mahabodhi Temple.

Conducted Tours (*see* : Patna)

Authorised Money Changers

- **Bank of India**, Hotel Embassy Ph 400950.
- **State Bank of India**, Mahayana Guest House Ph 400746.

Banks are open Monday to Friday 10 am - 2 pm. Saturday 10 am - 12 noon. Sunday closed. There are some private authorised money changers in the Mini Market who also accept and encash all credit cards.

Where to Stay

[B]odh Gaya offers accommodation at hotels, [g]uesthouses, dharmashalas and [m]onasteries.

[M]ost hotels accept major credit cards, yet [m]ake sure before you check in. The high-[en]d hotels have prayer halls, conference [an]d banquet facilities, business centres, [b]aby sitter, courier service, doctors on call, [la]undry, travel agencies, postal service, [ro]om service, parking facility. Most hotels [pr]ovide an extra bed for a payment of [ap]prox. 10% of the room rent. Most offer [di]scounts 20-50% in off season. There are [sp]ecial tariffs for groups. Service charge is [1]0% and luxury tax 7% is charged extra.

[L]uxury

[(A]bove Rs 1500 for a standard room with [si]ngle occupancy)

- **Bodhgaya Ashok** Ph 400790 Fax 400788
- **Sujata** Ph 400481 Fax 400515

[E]conomy

[R]s 750 and up to Rs 1500 for a standard [ro]om with single occupancy)

- **Buddha International** Ph 400506 Fax 400776
- **Embassy** Ph 400750
- **Mahayana Guest House** Ph 400744
- **Niranjana** Ph 400475 Fax 400873
- **Siddhartha Vihar** (Bihar Tourism Development Corporation) Ph 400445
- **Shashi International** Ph 400459 Fax 00483

[B]udget

[L]ess than Rs 750 for a standard room with [si]ngle occupancy)

- **Buddha Vihar** (BTDC) Ph 400445
- **Yatrik Tourist Bungalow** (BTDC) Ph 400445

[M]onasteries

[M]any of the monasteries in Bodh Gaya [pr]ovide simple accommodation at nominal [ra]tes. They usually give preference to [pil]grims and visitors from their respective [co]untries. Guests are expected to observe [so]me discipline and follow the rules and [re]gulations of the monasteries. If you wish [to] stay in a monastery, it is worth checking [ou]t by telephone.

- Birla Dharmashala Ph 400795
- Burmese Vihara and Guest House Ph 400721
- China Temple and Guest House Ph 400769
- Daijokyo Temple Ph 400407/400747
- GPL Tibetan Monastery Ph 400722

- Indosan Nipponji Japanese Temple Ph 400740/400743
- Korean Temple Ph 400512
- Lumbini Guest House Ph 400735 Fax 400777
- Mahabodhi Society Sri Lanka Rest House Ph 400742, 400797.
- New Bhutan Temple (Drukpa Monastery) Ph 400633.
- Royal Bhutan Monastery Ph 400710
- Royal Thailand Monastery Ph 400470
- Sechen Monastery Ph 400400
- Taiwan Temple 400502
- Tamang Nepalese Temple Ph 400802/400818
- Vietnam Temple and Guest House Ph 400733.

Where to Eat

Most hotels have their own multi cuisine restaurants. Some better restaurants are **Sujata Restaurant** at Bodh Gaya Ashok, **Amrapali Restaurant** and **Uruvela Garden Restaurant** at Hotel Niranjana, **Pavitra Restaurant** at Hotel Buddha International, **Siddhartha Restaurant** at Hotel Siddhartha Vihar. There are many wayside restaurants, which offer mixed Indian and European fare, the most popular being **Shiva** and **Kalpana**. A number of tent restaurants (dhabas) around the bus stand and Kalachakra ground sell fairly good Tibetan and Chinese food.

Where to Shop

The stalls outside the Mahabodhi Temple sell handcrafted soft stone images of Buddha, incense and candle stands, Bodhi leaves painted with Buddha or the Mahabodhi Temple.

Buddhist Institutions

- Asian Buddhist Culture Ph 400478
- Buddhist Bharat Thai Society Wat pa Ph 400845, 400528
- Dhammabodhi Vipasana Meditation Centre Ph 400437
- International Meditation Centre Ph 400707
- Mahabodhi Mahavihara Bodh Gaya Temple Management Committee Ph 400735 Fax 400777
- Root Institute for Culture and Wisdom
- Pragbodhi Temple (Sujata Academy) Ph 400764.

Most of these institutions offer meditation courses/programmes of different kinds. People who wish to contribute for the development of Bodh Gaya may contact the Secretary, Buddha Gaya Temple Management Committee, Bodh Gaya Library Building, Bodh Gaya.Ph 400735 Fax 400777.

RAJGIR

Arriving by Air

The nearest airport is Patna, 100 kms away. (*see*: Patna)

Arriving by Train

The nearest mainline is Bhakhtiyarpur, 54 kms, though the loop line connects Rajgir.

Important Train Connections

Train Nos/Train Names

❖ New Delhi-Bhagalpur via Bhakhtiyarpur
2392/2391 Magadh Vikramshila Express

❖ Delhi-Howrah via Bhakhtiyarpur
3040/3039 Howrah Delhi Janata Express

Travelling by Road

Rajgir is well connected by good roads to Patna, Gaya, Delhi and Calcutta. Private and State Roadways buses leave Patna every ten minutes for Biharsharif and touch Rajgir 25 kms away en route to Gaya. Matador vans, tempos and taxis are also available. Bihar Tourism organises conducted tours from Patna to Rajgir via Nalanda from its headquarters at Patna.

Ph 225411/222622 Fax 236218.

Important Road Distances

Bhakhtiyarpur	54 kms
Biharsharif	25 kms
Bodh Gaya	70 kms
Nalanda	11 kms
Patna	100 kms

Tourist Information Centres

● **Govt of Bihar Tourist Office,**
Kund Market

Where to Stay

There are a number of hotels in Rajgir mostly moderately priced.

Luxury

(Above Rs 1500 for a standard room with single occupancy)

● **Centaur Hokke** Ph 5245 Fax 5231

Bookings can be made in Calcutta at the Regional Marketing Office East
C/o Air India,
50 Chowringhee Road,
Poddar Centre, Calcutta 700071
Ph 2422356-59 Fax 2427875

Economy

(Rs 750 and above for a standard room with single occupancy).

● **Ajatshatru** (Tourist Bungalow II)
1/2 km from Kund Ph 25027

● **Gautam Vihar** (Tourist Bungalow I)
1 km from Kund Ph 25027

● **Siddhartha Kund** Ph 25216, 25352

Budget

(Less than Rs 750 for a standard room with single occupancy)

● **Mamta** opposite Digambar Jain Temple
Ph 25044. Fax 25210. Bookings can be made in Varanasi at Shabnam Travels
S-20/49 A-1, Baruna Bridge, Varanasi Cantt 221002(UP) and in Calcutta at Ramakrishna Travels, 39 Mahatma Gandhi Road, Calcutta 700009 Ph 3509199

● **Tathagat Vihar** (Tourist Bungalow III)
$^1/_2$ km from Kund Ph 25176

Where to Eat

Amber Restaurant (Tathagat Vihar Hotel) serves Indian, European and Chinese cuisine. Open 6 am-10 pm.
Centaur Hokke Hotel has an AC restaurant, which serves Indian, European and traditional Japanese food, and the Bar serves a variety of Indian and imported liquors. Prices are very steep. **Mamta Hotel & Restaurant** serves vegetarian Indian food. Non vegetarian meals are prepared only on order. Hotels also provide packed lunch for excursions. Season begins from October and ends in March. In the off season, hotels offer about 50% discount. 7% Luxury Tax is always levied.

NALANDA

Arriving by Air

The nearest airport is Patna 93 kms away. (*see* : Patna)

Arriving by Train

The nearest railhead connecting Nalanda is Bhakhtiyarpur, which is at a distance of 38 kms on the loopline connecting with the Delhi-Howrah mainline. (*see* : Rajgir)

Travelling by Road

Nalanda is connected by road to Patna, Rajgir, Gaya, Delhi and Calcutta. From Patna private and State Transport buses leave for Biharsharif every ten minutes and touch Nalanda en route to Gaya. Tempos and taxis are also available from Biharsharif. Bihar Tourism organises

xcursions from its headquarters in Patna.
ee : Patna)

Important Road Distances

Bhakhtiyarpur	38 kms
Bodh Gaya	80 kms
Patna	90 kms
Rajgir	11 kms

ourist Information Centres

● **Govt of Bihar Tourist Information Office**,
Bargaon, Nava Nalanda, near Bus Stand.

Where to Stay

urists prefer to stay in Rajgir, 10 kms
way. **The Guest House** in the Nava
alanda Mahavihara and the **Burmese
est House** are not open for general
urists, but may provide overnight
ccommodation on request. Visitors are
dvised to carry packed lunch and drinking
ater. Nalanda can be ideally covered in a
ay trip.

VAISHALI

Arriving by Air

atna is the nearest airport 63 kms away.
ee : Patna)

Arriving by Train

he nearest railhead is at Hajipur, 35 kms
way.

mportant Train Connections

Train Nos/Train Names

New Delhi-Barauni via Hajipur
2554/2553 Vaishali Express

Travelling by Road

aishali is connected by a good road to
atna via Hajipur.

Important Road Distances

Hajipur	35 kms
Kushinagar	280kms
Muzaffarpur	36 kms
Patna	56 kms

ourist Information Centres

● **Tourist Bungalow**
Govt of Bihar Tourist Information Office
Ph 85425

Where to Stay

Most people prefer to make a day trip from
Patna, since the accommodation available
here is limited.

Budget

(less than Rs 750 for a standard room with
single occupancy)

● **Tourist Bungalow** Ph 85425

SARNATH

Arriving by Air

Nearest airport is Varanasi Airport at
Babatpur, 30 kms from Sarnath.
(*see*: Varanasi)

Arriving by Train

Nearest railway stations are Varanasi,
12 kms, and Mughal Sarai Junction,
15 kms. (*see*: Varanasi)

Important Train Connections

(*see*: Varanasi)

Travelling by Road

Sarnath is well connected to Varanasi and
other cities of Uttar Pradesh.
(*see*: Varanasi)

Important Road Distances

Varanasi	10 kms

(*see* : Varanasi for other
distances)

Tourist Information Centres

● **Tourist Bungalow, Govt. of UP**,
Sarnath Ph 342515

● **Tourist Information Counter, Govt. of India**,
Babatpur Airport Ph 343472

Conducted Tours

(*see* : Varanasi)

Authorised Money Changers

● **State Bank of Travancore**
Ashapur, Ph 355035

● **Canara Bank** Ph 385038

● **Central Bank** Ph 385309

Hospitals & Nursing Homes

✚ Dr. Baijnath Hospital, Sarnath
Ph 385238

✚ Government Hospital, Sarnath

Communications

✉ **Post Office**, Sarnath Ph 385013

Where to Stay

It is best to stay in Varanasi and take a taxi to Sarnath for the day, since there are very few hotels in Sarnath.

Budget

(Less than Rs 750 for a standard room with single occupancy)

- **Chitra Vihar** Ph 386280
- **Forest Dept Guest House** Ph 387841
- **Golden Buddha Guest** House Ph 387933
- **Mahabodhi Guest House** Ph 385595
- **Mrigadava** (UP Tourism) Ph 386965.

KUSHINAGAR

Arriving by Air

Varanasi Airport at Babatpur, 280 kms away, is the nearest airport (*see* : Varanasi)

Arriving by Train

Gorakhpur Railway Station, 51 kms from Kushinagar, is the most convenient as it is well connected to all the major cities in India. Gorakhpur also has a fully computerised reservation centre.

Important Train Connections

Train Nos/Train Names

- ❖ Delhi-Barauni
  2554/2553 Vaishali Exp
- ❖ Dadar-Gorakhpur
  1027/1028 Kashi Exp
- ❖ Delhi-Darbangha
  4674/4673 Shaheed Exp
- ❖ Mumbai-Gorakhpur
  1015/1016 Kushinagar Exp
- ❖ Ahmedabad-Gorakhpur via Lucknow
  5045/5046 Ahmedabad Gorakhpur Exp
- ❖ Gorakhpur-Howrah via Patna
  5048/5047 Purvanchal Exp
- ❖ Delhi-Guwahati
  5610/5609 Avadh Assam Exp

Travelling by Road

Important Road Distances

Gorakhpur	51 kms
Kapilavastu (Piprahwa)	148 kms
Lumbini via Gorakhpur	176 kms
Sarnath	261 kms
Sravasti	274 kms
Vaishali	280 kms

Bus

The main bus terminus in Gorakhpur is a three minute walk from the railway station. Main Bus Stand, Gorakhpur Ph 332893

Tourist Information Centres

- **Govt of UP Tourist Bureau**, Buddha Marg, Kushinagar. Medical facilities of a basic kind are available at Government Community Health Centre, Deoria Road.

Banks

- **Central Bank of India**, Kasya Road, Kushinagar
- **State Bank of India**, Kasya Road, Kushinaga Ph 05563-7124

Important Phone Numbers

District Magistrate, Padrauna
Ph **22010**, SDM, Kasia Ph **2040**

Communications

✉ Sub Post Office, Main Crossing,

Where to Stay

Luxury

(Above Rs 1500 for a standard room with single occupancy)

- **Lotus Nikko** Ph 7139

Budget

(Less than Rs 750 for a standard room with single occupancy)

- **Pathik Niwas** UP Govt Tourist Bungalow Ph 7138

There are also other options for staying in Kushinagar:

- Chandramani Bhikshu Dharamshala
- Hindu Birla Buddha Dharamshala
- International Guest House
- Nepali Dharamshala

At Gorakhpur:

Travellers looking for good hotels can stay at one of the hotels in Gorakhpur, which a all in the Economy range.

- **Marina** Ph 337630
- **President** Golghar Ph 337654
- **Upavan** Nepal Road

Where to Eat

Pathik Niwas has a reasonably good mult cuisine restaurant. There are not many other restaurants in Kushinagar.

LUMBINI (NEPAL)

Most tourists prefer to travel by car from the Indian side, breaking the journey at Sonauli, 27 kms away, on the Indian side of the international border. For entering Nepal, a tax of Nepalese Rs 300 has to be paid at the border for a one-day permit. Getting the permit is a cumbersome process, and may take around two hours. People from India and Bhutan do not need permits but others do.

Arriving by Air

Nearest airport is Varanasi (323 kms) and Bhairawha, Nepal (13 kms).

Arriving by Train

The nearest railhead is Gorakhpur, 123 kms away via Sonauli (see : Gorakhpur)

Travelling by Road

Buses ply up to the Indian side of the border, from where the passengers have to disembark and take another bus after crossing the border check post.

Important Road Distances

Gorakhpur via Sonauli	123 kms
Kapilavastu (Piprahwa) via Sonauli	93 kms
Kushinagar via Gorakhpur	176 kms
Sonauli	27 kms

Important Phone Numbers

Lumbini International Research Institute Ph **80175**

Korean Monastery Ph **80123**

Tibetan Monastery Ph **80172**

Where to Stay

Most travellers from India take a day-permit to Lumbini and prefer to spend the night at Gorakhpur or at Sonauli.

At Sonauli:

○ **Niranjana** (UP Tourism) Ph 05522-38201

At Lumbini:

○ **Lumbini Hokke** in the Luxury category is the best option in Lumbini Ph 20236

○ **Sri Lanka Pilgrims Guest House** has very basic accommodation Ph 20009

KAPILAVASTU
(PIPRAHWA)

Arriving by Air

Varanasi 312 kms away, is the nearest airport. It is a long journey and the traveller is advised to take adequate care.
(see : Varanasi)

Arriving by Train

Siddharthnagar Railway Station, situated at a distance of 20 kms is the nearest rail link, but it is not well served. Gorakhpur, 97 kms away, is the best alternative.

Travelling by Road

Kapilavastu is well linked by good all weather roads to Gorakhpur and other towns of UP.

Important Road Distances

Gorakhpur	97 kms
Kushinagar	148 kms
Lucknow	308 kms
Lumbini via Sonauli	93 kms
Sravasti	147 kms
Varanasi	32 kms

Tourist Information Centres

○ **Tourist Office, Govt of UP**, Siddharthnagar. Basic medical facilities are available at the Primary Health Care Centre at Berdpur, 8.5 kms away.

Important Phone Numbers

District Magistrate Siddharthnagar **Ph 2333/2180**

Police Station Siddharthnagar **Ph 400741**

Communications

✉ Berdpur Post Office, 8.5 kms away

Where to Stay

Accommodation is likely to be available at either of the following places. However, it is best to avoid staying in Kapilavastu unless absolutely essential.

○ Sri Lankan Temple Mahinda Vihara, Pachan Gawa, Ph 05544-22231

○ Rahi Motel (UPSTDC) village Birha, 1 km away from Kapilavastu.

SRAVASTI

Arriving by Air

The nearest airport is Lucknow, which is at a distance of 151 kms.

Lucknow is connected by air to Delhi, Mumbai, Calcutta and Patna.

Domestic Airlines Offices

Indian Airlines
Mahatma Gandhi Road
Ph 220927/224618
Airport Ph 435401/436132

Sahara India Airlines
7 Kapurthala Complex
Aliganj Road
Ph 321253/325288
Fax 3782000
Airport Ph 437771

Jet Airways
6 Park Road
Ph 239612/239614
Fax 239613
Airport Ph 434009/434010

Air connections from Lucknow

▶ Lucknow-Delhi
   IC 884 Indian Airlines Mo/Th

▶ Lucknow-Delhi
   IC 836 Indian Airlines Daily

▶ Lucknow-Delhi
   9W 742 Jet Airways, Daily

▶ Lucknow - Delhi
   S2 514 Sahara India Airlines Daily

▶ Lucknow-Patna-Calcutta
   IC 7411 Indan Airlines Mo/We/Fr/Su

▶ Lucknow-Mumbai
   9W 376 Jet Airways Daily

▶ Lucknow-Mumbai
   S2 907 Sahara India Airlines Daily

Arriving by Train

Balrampur, 19 kms away, is the nearest railway station. Most prefer to arrive from Lucknow or Varanasi. (*see also* : Varanasi)

Important Train Connections for Lucknow

Train Nos/Train Names

❖ New Delhi-Lucknow
   2003/2004 Shatabdi Exp

❖ Patna-New Delhi via Lucknow
   2309/2310 Rajdhani Exp

❖ New Delhi-Barauni via Lucknow
   2553/2554 Vaishali Exp

❖ New Delhi-Lucknow
   4229/4230 Lucknow Mail

Important Train Connections from Balrampur

❖ Gonda Jn-Gorakhpur via Balrampur
   5322/5321 Kapilvastu Express (metre gauge)

Travelling by Road

There are frequent bus services from Balrampur and also from Lucknow and Varanasi.

Important Road Distances

Bahraich	47 kms
Balrampur	19 kms
Gonda	50 kms
Kapilavastu via Naugarh	147 kms
Lucknow via Bahraich	151 kms
Varanasi	260 kms

Tourist Information Centres

● **Govt of UP Tourist Bureau**,
   Balrampur
   Fax 221776.

Important Phone Numbers

District Magistrate, Bahraich
Ph **05252-32401**

Where to Stay

Luxury

(Above Rs 1500 for a standard room with single occupancy)

● **Lotus Nikko Sravasti** Ph 65291.
   Reservations have to be done from Delhi at Lotus Travels, Rajendra Place, New Delhi
   Ph 5766559/5735073

Budget

(Less than Rs 750 for a standard room with single occupancy)

● **Sri Lanka Ramayath Guest House**
   Ph 65245,65277

Accommodation is also available, on request at the following monasteries:

● Burmese Monastery Ph 65244
● Chinese Monastery Ph 65243
● Sri Lanka Monastery (Anand Bodhi Society)
   Ph 65245

Balrampur, 19 kms away, offers reasonable options for the traveller to stay, and most of them are in the Economy range.

● **Maya** Ph 32507 Fax 32508
● **Pathik** Balrampur Ph 32265
● **Tourism Bungalow**, UP Tourism,
   Balrampur Ph 32456

Important Addresses

Asian Buddhist Culture
Bodh Gaya. Ph 400478

Central Institute of Higher Tibetan Studies
PO Sarnath, Varanasi 221007

Council for Religious and Cultural Affairs
Gangchen Kyishong
Dharamsala, Dist Kangra. Ph 21343

His Holiness, the Dalai Lama
Thekchen Choeling, McLeodganj
Dharamsala
Ph 01892-22343, 24879 Fax 22457

Bureau of HH The Dalai Lama, Delhi
DA Ring Road, Lajpat Nagar IV
New Delhi 110024 Ph 6414888
Fax 6461914

Delhi Nalanda Institute
C-19 20 Mehrauli Institutional Area
New Delhi 110016 Ph 6960767

Department of Buddhist Studies
University of Delhi, New Delhi
Ph 7257725 Ext 218

Dhammabodhi Vipassana Centre
Bodh Gaya Ph 400437

Indian Museum
Chowringhee, Calcutta 700013

Institute of Buddhist Dialectics
Thekchen Choeling, McLeodganj
Dharamsala Ph 21215/ 21252

International Meditation Centre
Bodh Gaya Ph 400707

Ladakh Bauddha Vihara
Bela Road
New Delhi 110054 Ph 3970455

Library of Tibetan Works and Archives
Gangchen Kyishong
Dharamsala Ph 22467

Mahabodhi Mahavihara
Budddha Gaya Temple Management Committee
Bodh Gaya Ph 400735 Fax 400777

Mahabodhi Society of India
4A Bankim Chatterjee Street
Calcutta 700073

Mahabodi Society of India
Mandir Marg (Next to Birla Mandir)
New Delhi 110001 Ph 3363328

Men Tsee Khang
Tibetan Medical and Astrological Institute
3 Jaipur Estate, Nizamuddin East
New Delhi Ph 4698503/4635039

Namgyal Institute of Tibetology
Gangtok, Sikkim

National Museum of India
1 Janpath New Delhi 110001
Ph 3792217

Nechung Drayangling Monastery
Gangchen Kyishong
Dharamsala, Dist Kangra Ph 22791

Norbulinka Institute
Dharamsala, Dist. Kangra
Ph 23522, 23575

Paljor Publications
D-39 Jangpura Extension
New Delhi 110014
Ph 4310866, 4312416

Potala Travels
Antriksh Bhavan, 1011 22 KG Marg
New Delhi 110001 Ph 3723284

Pragbodhi Temple (Sujata Academy)
Bodh Gaya Ph 400964

Root Institute for Culture and Wisdom
Bodh Gaya Ph 400714

Rumtek Monastery
Dharma Chakra Centre
PO Rumtek via Ranipul, Gangtok 737135
Sikkim Ph 2363

Tawang Monastery
Thupten Gompa
PO Tawang, District Kameng
Arunachal Pradesh

Tibet House
1 Institutional Area, Lodi Road
New Delhi Ph 4611515

Tibetan Institute of Performing Arts
McLeodganj, Dharamsala Ph 21478/ 21433

Tibetan Medical and Astrological Institute
Khara Dhanda Road, Dharamsala

Tushita Mahayana Meditation Centre
C-259 Defence Colony
New Delhi Ph 6513400 Fax 4692963

Tushita Retreat Centre
McLeodganj, Dharamsala
Ph 21866 Fax 21246

World Buddha Foundation
Bodh Gaya, Ph 400449

In the Footsteps of the Buddha

Shantum Seth, a student of the Buddhist
Zen Master Thich Nhat Hanh conducts
exclusive pilgrimages 'In the Footsteps of
the Buddha'. The group visits the sites
associated with the Buddha's life, practising
meditation, travelling mindfully and hearing
stories about the Buddha and his teachings.

For further information and brochure, please
contact:

309-B Sector 15A, NOIDA 201301, India
Ph 91521520, 91532641
Fax 91521520

GLOSSARY

Abhidharma (Abhidamma) Pitaka - the third *Pitaka* (basket) or collection of Buddhist canon, dealing with metaphysics.

ahimsa - concept of non-violence evolved by Buddhists and Jains as opposed to *himsa* or violence.

anagarika - literally, homeless; originally an epithet for a Buddhist monk. Name adopted by David Hewavitarane, the Sri Lankan lay Buddhist who dedicated his life to the revival of Buddhism.

Amitabha (Japanese: *Amida*) - the primary Bodhisattva in the northern Mahayana pantheon.

anatman (*annata*) - the doctrine of 'not-soul' or 'not self' (*anatta*), preached by the Buddha.

Arhat - an enlightened person, who has extinguished craving and achieved *Nirvana*, the ideal of the Theravada school of Buddhism.

ashram - hermitage

atman - the self or individual soul in the ancient Hindu tradition (see: *karma*).

Avalokiteshwara - the Mahayana Bodhisattva of compassion. Known as *Chenrezi* in Tibetan and regarded as the protector of Tibet. His reincarnations are the successive Dalai Lamas.

bhikshu (*bhikku*) - literally, a beggar; the name by which the Buddha called his followers. Thus, a Buddhist monk is called *Bhikshu*.

bhikshuni (*bhikkuni*) - Buddhist nun.

Bodhi - Enlightenment, realisation. Also called *samma sambodhi*. The pipal tree (*ficus religiosia*) came to be known as the Bodhi or Bo tree after the Buddha attained Enlightenment under this tree at Bodh Gaya.

Bodhisattva - the ideal of the Mahayana tradition, an individual who delays his own Enlightenment in order to lead other sentient beings to deliverance.

Brahma - the God of creation in the Hindu pantheon.

Brahman / Brahmin - the priestly caste and the highest in the Hindu caste hierarchy (see: *Varna*).

Brahmi - the script used for writing inscriptions by the Mauryas. The inscriptions on Emperor Ashoka's pillars in most parts of India were in Prakrit language, Brahmi script.

chhatra - the umbrella on top of the stupa. A traditional honorific symbol.

chaitya - a sacred place; most commonly used as halls of worship.

chakra - literally, wheel; a recurring motif in Buddhist art; a symbol of the Buddha's teaching.

deva - gods in Hindu mythology.

Devraj Indra - the king of gods in Hindu mythology

Dharma - translated variously as the natural law, the truth, the teaching of enlightened ones, religion, social order, morality, righteousness and so on. Used in this book to refer to the teachings of the Buddha.

Dhammapada - religious book containing the sayings of the Buddha

Dharma (*dhamma*) *yatra* - the pilgrimage to the four holy places associated with the life of Lord Buddha - Lumbini, Bodh Gaya, Sarnath and Kushinagar.

gompa - Tibetan for monastery.

guru - a teacher, one who shows the way.

Hinayana - The lesser vehicle, referred to as such by the practitioners of Mahayana tradition, because the followers of the older Hinayana school aspired for individual enlightenment. Also known as the Theravada.

Jain - a religious community founded by Lord Mahavira (see: Mahavira).

Jataka - the 547 Jatakas or Birth Stories are allegorical tales relating the Buddha's previous births.

karma - literally, action; the consequences resulting from previous action; the doctrine of *karma* governs human and other beings. The doctrine of *karma* teaches that all action involves a build-up in the soul of spiritual merit or demerit. Good action leads to favourable rebirth, while bad actions, whether or not intentional, leads to unfavourable rebirth. According to Buddhists the only genuine escape from the cycle of birth and rebirth is *Nirvana*. According to Brahmanical Hinduism the individual soul or self (*atman*) must purify itself of its *karma* and merge with the universal spirit (*brahman*).

Kshatriya - the warrior caste and the second in the Hindu caste hierarchy (see: *Varna*).

lama - a teacher or guru in the Tibetan Buddhist tradition. The title *Dalai Lama*, literally, means the Ocean of Wisdom.

Mahavira - the founder of the Jain religion, Mahavira, was a contemporary of the Buddha, and their lives had striking similarities. Mahavira was born as Prince Vardhaman in a royal family at Vaishali in 540 BC. He married Yashodhara and after the birth of a daughter, left home at the age of thirty. More than a decade of wandering, practising meditation and self-austerities led to his attaining Kaivalya Jnana (supreme knowledge). Mahavira rejected the Brahmanical Hindu notion of religion and the practice of rituals. He taught that leading a non-violent and ethical life would negate bad *karma* and lead to deliverance. Though it never became a world religion, Jainism has always maintained its presence in India, unlike Buddhism.

Mahavihara - monastic university.

Mahayana - literally, the great vehicle; the later school in Buddhism, its emphasis is on the deliverance of all sentient beings for which the Bodhisattva strives.

mandala - ritual drawings which represent the cosmos; in architecture, the *mandala* theory meant a group of buildings arrranged at cardinal points surrounding a sacred central point.

Manjusri - a Bodhisattva who dispels ignorance.

mantra - sacred syllables, whose recitation is said to bring supernatural powers.

Mara - the personification of evil; the temptor in Buddhist mythology, who tried unsuccessfully to distract the Buddha in his meditation.

mudra - gestures of the hand, each of which has a meaning, a symbolic language.

Nirvana - simplest translation, Enlightenment; it is also peace; the death of craving; detachment; extinction. *Nirvana* is a condition to be experienced by a person who has eliminated the notion of self.

Om mani padme hum - Om, the jewel is in the lotus. The powerful mantra of Avalokiteshwara.

Pali - the Indo-Aryan language in which the Buddha spoke and in which the Buddhist canon was originally composed.

Parinirvana - the final extinction from *samsara*, the cycle of birth, life and death.

Pitaka - literally, basket; the three *Pitakas* in Pali which constitute the Buddhist canonical texts. The three *pitakas* (*Tripitaka*) are the *Vinaya*, *Sutra* and *Abhidharma Pitaka*.

poornima - full moon.

prajna - knowledge or wisdom. Prajnaparamita, means perfection of wisdom; the name of the goddess personifying wisdom in Mahayana tradition.

puja - the chief mode of worship in Hindu tradition.

punya (*punna*) - spiritual merit, accumulated by leading a blemish free life and doing good deeds; leading to a favourable rebirth.

Sakyamuni - another name of Lord Buddha. Sakyamuni literally means the saint of the Sakyas, the clan to which the Buddha was born.

samsara - the endless cycle of birth and rebirth.

185

Sangha - the Buddhist community of monks and nuns, founded by the Buddha in Sarnath.

Sanskrit - classical Indian language; language in which the Hindu religious texts were written. *Samskrata* literally means refined as opposed to *Prakrit* which means unrefined.

siddha - yogic master or spiritual adept in *Tantra*.

stupa - a dome-shaped Buddhist reliquary. Known as *chorten* in Tibetan.

sutra (*sutta*) - aphoristic scripture: said to be the original teachings of the Buddha.

tangkha - Tibetan Buddhist religious painting on fabric.

tantra - a ritual path to salvation, derived from the *tantras*, a class of esoteric religious texts in both Hindu and Buddhist traditions.

Tara - female saviour in Mahayana tradition.

Tathagata - an epithet used for the Buddha; literally, the thus gone, or the thus come.

Theravada (Sanskrit: *Sthaviravada*) - path of the elders (see: *Hinayana*).

Theragatha and *Therigatha* - literature composed by the *bhikshus* and *bhikshunis*, respectively.

Tirthankara - preceptors in the Jain religion. Mahavira was the twentyfourth in the lineage of Tirthankaras.

torana - an arched entrance.

tripitaka - (see: *pitaka*).

triratna - three jewels of Buddhism, the *Buddha*, the *Dharma* and the *Sangha*.

upasaka (female: *upasika*) - lay Buddhist follower.

Upanishad - philosophical treatises, composed as appendices to the Vedas.

vada - literally, debate; usually accepted form of conflict resolution in ancient India between philosophers.

vajra (Tibetan *dorje*) - thunderbolt or diamond, a Mahayana symbol of the Absolute. *Vajrayana*, literally, the vehicle of the *vajra*; the great movement in Mahayana Buddhism in Tibet. The four main sects of Vajrayana in Tibet are *Nyingmapa*, *Sakyapa*, *Kagyupa*,and *Gelugpa*, in the chronological order of development.

varna - literally, colour; a term used to refer to the four castes (*varnas*) i.e., Brahmins, Kshatriyas, Vaishyas and Shudras in the hierarchical Hindu social order.

vassavasa - in Pali *vassa* means the rainy season and *vasa* means residence. *Vassavasa* means a rain retreat for the *Sangha*.

Veda - earliest and holiest of the Hindu religious texts (c 1500 BC - 600 BC); the wisdom contained in the Vedas is said to be divinely revealed.

Vinaya Pitaka - code of Buddhist monastic discipline as set in Pali.

yaksha - mythical beings of pre-Buddhist Indian origin associated with fertility cults; *yakshas* and their female form, *yakshis*, are prominently displayed on early stupas where they signify prosperity and abundance.

yantra - sacred diagram used for ritual purposes.

yogi - a practitioner of yoga, a classical Indian philosophy of science and enlightenment.

Zen - meditative school of Buddhism flowering in Japan, based on intuitive insight and sudden enlightenment. Originally known as *Dhyana* in India and *Chan* in China, from where it spread to Japan.

Note: The words in parenthesis are in Pali unless otherwise indicated

FURTHER READING

Literary Sources

Dhammapada (trans.), Ven. Narada Maha Thera (Calcutta, 1991).

Jataka Tales (retold), Ethel Beswick (London, 1956).

The Jatakas (ed.), E.B.Cowell (New Delhi, 1979)

Vinaya Pitaka, Sutta Pitaka, Abhidhamma Pitaka, Mahayana Texts in Max Mueller (ed.), Sacred Books of The East (separate volumes) translated into English from original Pali (New Delhi, reprint 1993).

History, Culture, Art & Philosophy

Aitken, Molly Emma, Meeting the Buddha (New York, 1995).

Bapat, P.V.(ed.), 2500 Years of Buddhism (New Delhi, 1997).

Basham, A.L., The Wonder that was India (London, 1985).

Bechert, H. and Gombrich, R.(eds.), The World Of Buddhism (New York, 1984).

Behl, Benoy, The Ajanta Caves (London, 1998).

Brown, Percy, Indian Architecture - Hindu and Buddhist Periods (Bombay, 1996).

Carus, Paul, The Gospel of Buddha (London, 1997).

Conze, Edward (ed.), Buddhist Texts through the Ages (New York, 1973).

Coomaraswamy, Ananda, History of Indian and Indonesian Art (New York, 1988).

Dalai Lama, His Holiness the XIVth Dalai Lama, The Power Of Compassion (Delhi, 1998).

Dasgupta, S.B., An Introduction to Tantric Buddhism (Berkeley, 1974).

Dutt, Sukumar, Buddhist Monks and Monasteries in India (London, 1962).

Eliade, M.(ed.), The Encyclopedia of Religion (New York, 1987).

Fergusson, James, History of Indian and Eastern Architecture, Vols I & II (Delhi, 1994).

Fisher, Robert E., Buddhist Art and Architecture (London, 1993).

Grunwedel, Albert, Buddhist Art in India (Varanasi, 1974).

Hessig, W., The Religions of Mongolia (Berkeley, 1979).

Humphreys, C.A., Popular Dictionary Of Buddhism (London, 1976).

Lowenstein, Tom, The Vision of The Buddha (London, 1996).

Michell, G., The Penguin Guide to the Monuments of India, Volume1 (London, 1989).

Narain, A.K. (ed.), Studies in the History Of Buddhism (Delhi, 1980).

Norbu, Dawa & Choedon, Yeshi, Tibet (New Delhi, !998).

Oldenberg, Hermann, Buddha: His Life, His Doctrine, His Order (Delhi, 1997).

Radakrishnan, S. & Moore, C., A Sourcebook in Indian Philosophy (Princeton,1973).

Rahula, W., What The Buddha Taught (London, 1990).

Rajesh, M.N., The Buddhist Monastery (New Delhi, 1998).

Rhys Davids, T.W., Buddhism (Delhi, 1997).

Shearer, Alistair, Buddha The Intelligent Heart (London, 1987).

Suzuki, D.T., Japanese Spirituality (Tokyo, 1972).

Thapar, Romila, A History of India (London, 1974).

Tharu, Susie and Lalita, K.(ed.), Women Writing in India, Vol. I (New Delhi, 1995).

Thich Naht Hanh, Being Peace (Paris, 1989).

Tucci, G.,The Religions of Tibet (Berkeley, 1980).

Warder, A.K., Indian Buddhism (Oxford, 1963).

Waterstone, Richard, India Belief And Ritual (London, 1995).

Wood, E., Zen Dictionary (Tokyo,1972).

INDEX

INDEX

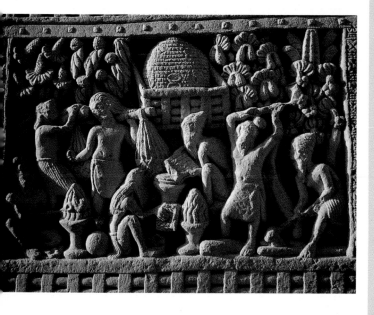

NOTES

NOT TO SCALE